AMERICA'S CAPACITY TO GOVERN

AMERICA'S
CAPACITY
to GOVERN

SOME PRELIMINARY THOUGHTS
FOR PROSPECTIVE ADMINISTRATORS

GEORGE A. GRAHAM

1 9 6 0

UNIVERSITY OF ALABAMA PRESS

342.73
G76a

To

ALLEN and MARTHA

Preface

A LISTENER HAS A RIGHT TO KNOW WHAT a lecturer is trying to accomplish. He who reads essays which were given as lectures, lacking the listener's opportunity to ask probing questions, has a double right to know what the essayist is up to. If the author's purpose is honorable and his method straightforward, he also has something to gain in putting his cards on the table at the outset. This I shall try to do in these rather personal introductory remarks.

Why would any prudent person tackle so difficult a subject as "America's Capacity to Govern"? It is almost preposterous. More particularly, why would I attempt to discuss this subject when I am neither a philosopher nor a scientist? (Not a behavioral scientist, either, although I would be proud to wear that label.) I am only a "political scientist," a professional student of politics, for most of my life a university teacher in an "ivy college," where the overriding compulsion is to get at the truth for its own sake without gloss or glamour—and to help other students to do so. I have also had the benefit of limited periods of service in government, and of more frequent periods of concentrated investigation of governmental problems, usually of a practical nature.

This is the immediate experience on which I now draw.

The background is also relevant to understanding my temerity in taking up the subject of these lectures. My professional life coincides with the boom of the Twenties, the great depression, the New Deal, World War II, and the strange new world that has emerged, unforeseen and unpredicted. This is an era in which the extremes of want and wealth, now on a world-wide scale of comparison, have become more appalling. A new empire built on ancient lines of authority and domination has risen while other empires have been disintegrating. At the same time, elsewhere, fanatical nationalism has revived, and still elsewhere people would now welcome a reasonable internationalism if it were available. Nation states have risen quickly, and fallen even faster. Parliamentary governments and dictatorships have changed places restlessly and not infrequently on the world stage. In these actions there is the clash of philosophies and personalities as well as the conflict of movements and forces.

These events raise the question of capacity to govern naturally enough. For professional students of politics these have been intellectually stimulating years. Efforts to penetrate the secrets of political power or to find an answer to the riddle of political change have accelerated. The search for natural laws has revived although the nomenclature is new, and the methods of inquiry more varied. Each student of politics in his own way must react to the challenge of political life and attempt to understand it. Few questions which are fundamental in importance can transcend that of capacity to govern.

A political scientist can hardly avoid the subject in some form.

On two occasions, through the generosity of Princeton University, the Rockefeller Foundation, and the University of Hawaii, I have had an opportunity to think about the nature of capacity to govern and how it can be measured. In the effort to think systematically, my inventory of significant factors grew larger and larger, and my analysis of their effects became more and more complex. It was evident that although some day I might have a rather complete list of factors which determine capacity to govern, and even if my weighting of these factors might by some chance be valid, the total analysis would be almost as complex—and obscure—as political reality itself. This discovery was discouraging, especially since it was obvious that my failure to see it in the beginning was a measure of my own haste and naiveté. The direction of my inquiry then turned to the more modest purpose of seeing whether I could find a simplified approach, or could concentrate on a few of the factors in such a way as to aid understanding even at the cost of comprehensiveness. This I tried to do in the lectures given in Tuscaloosa, Alabama, in November, 1958, to the students of the Southern Regional Training Program then at the University of Alabama.

Although the lectures began where the philosophers do, with man and society, I turned not to the philosophers but to the findings of research to discover whether the scientists in the past century of productive effort have revealed man as more or less capable than the philosophers thought he was for self-government.

The first lecture, "Is Man a Political Animal?" presents my findings. Here I should like to explain why I went directly to the researchers, particularly, the psychologists, rather than to my fellow political scientists who have written much and wisely on man's political behavior. The basic explanation is simple: it was easier for me to do so. Many years ago I had the privilege of studying with a distinguished university teacher, William Cornell Casey, then at the University of Illinois. He made students of government aware of the relevance to political science of the works of Watson, Pavlov, the experimental psychologists, and the sociologists. Because of this early training, it was easier for me to draw my own conclusions from psychological and social data than to rely upon the behaviorists in political science. This is in no way a reflection on their distinguished work.

The reader should understand that what I have done is merely to review as a layman some of the better substantiated findings and more persuasive conclusions of the scientists. I have not discovered anything new in psychology, nor have I attempted to go into controversial areas of that discipline. Most of the basic points which I have considered in the first lecture are so well substantiated and so widely accepted that I have not thought it necessary to argue their validity.

The second lecture, "Is Democracy Viable?" is essentially a continuation of the first. The center of attention simpy shifts from man as an individual to men in groups. The conclusion to be drawn from the first two lectures is that democratic society and democratic government are consistent with man's nature, and probably a better medium for full realization of his capacities than other societies. But democracy is not for this reason more probable. Rationality and good will, woven into learned patterns of behavior, are *achievements,* not static qualities of man. They are the product of deliberately exercised capacities. Democracy as an achievement is natural rather than contrary to nature, but no more natural in this sense than is an authoritarian society.

How can capacities to govern democratically be measured? There will be government in some form, come what may, but will it be democratic? Can America survive and will it continue to achieve both democracy and progress? My answers to these questions are contained in lectures three, four, and five: "How Can Capacity to Govern Be Measured?"; "Leadership and the Public Service"; and "How Good Is the Best Society?"

In discussing the critical element of leadership in the fourth lecture, I have given some attention to the practical problem of providing an adequate supply of high-capacity leadership in the national administration. I trust that this concern with an immediate problem will not offend the more philosophic readers of this essay. It may serve to illustrate the hard fact that governmental success depends as much upon coping with immediate and practical difficulties as upon having an adequate philosophy. I shall be interested in your reaction to the emphasis in these lectures upon the importance of the combined exercise of capacities for rationality and good will and upon the continuing need for the heroic act—sacrifice. Does it make sense to you, or nonsense? Is it questionable, or is it a simple truth which you have understood all along?

I am tempted to suggest one additional thought, although it is not part of the argument of the lectures. With Mr. Doolittle I would say that, in governing, it is helpful, and a joyous thing, to have "a little bit o' luck."

I would be less than candid if I did not tell you that I have had more than my share of that important element in life. For a good many years Princeton University provided for me an intellectual home that was close to the optimum for thoughtful study of politics. Princeton also provided two leaves of absence from teaching for my struggles with the subject of governing capacity. One of these the Rockefeller Foundation very generously extended from one term to a full academic year. The University of Hawaii first gave me the opportunity, and the courage, to try out some of these ideas upon graduate students, a very essential and useful step. The Brookings Institution, when I was facing a deadline unprepared, made it possible for me to get the "preliminary thoughts" of these lectures down on paper. And finally the University of Alabama provided the stimulus of an intelligent university audience which I found to be most sympathetic and hospitable.

I can only hope for one more "bit o' luck," that you, thoughtful reader, will bear in mind the limited objective of these lectures: (1) not research, but an interpretation of work done by others; (2) not new and complex formulations, but a somewhat simpler way of viewing a very complex world; (3) not final judgments that you are asked to accept, but preliminary thoughts that may perhaps encourage you to look afresh at the realities amidst which we live, to understand the political world better, and to reach your own, for you, more valid conclusions.

If you are a sophisticated social scientist who fully understands "American democracy," go no further; this small book is not for you. You are already away ahead of me. This is a book for beginners based on limited knowledge, limited insight, and limited ability even to begin to answer the most important questions. A most intelligent and thoughtful reader of the essays in manuscript form, moreover, has taken me to task rather severely for raising questions without answering them. I feel that his demand for answers may be too immediate and precise, and I wish that he could be more patient with my discourse. But his criticism may be entirely correct. If you have the answers yourself or if you expect my preliminary thoughts to be "answers," you will be disappointed and perhaps irritated. I must warn you to proceed at your own risk.

For those who are beginning their careers in public administration, or who are only beginning to develop their analytic ideas about American society, and who are curious to see what another has to say on this important subject, I would say one more word. I am, of course, indebted to a wide variety of researchers and scholars for help. I am not aware that what I have to say here is new or original, and in the selection of ideas and data presented I doubtless am not conscious of the origin or the avenue of my acquaintance with very many items. This great indebtedness to others I can acknowledge only in a general way as a debt to the culture in which I live.

Before permitting the University of Alabama to go ahead with its plan to publish the lectures, however, I asked a number of friends and colleagues to read and criticize the manuscript in full or in part. Their response was most generous. Among them were three political scientists, three psychologists, an economist, an administrator, and one, who, to put it conservatively, is ranked among the "behavioral scientists." Nearly all of these men also have had substantial experience in government, and all may fairly be said to be serious and informed students of the American scene. I am almost reluctant to mention their names lest in some way they be compromised. Let me clear them at once by saying that I did not adopt all of the suggestions made, and that on various points some of these friends are not in agreement with me. They are not in any way committed to the views expressed in these essays. I am, however, most grateful for their reading of the essays and for their penetrating and helpful comments. They are: Bernard Berelson, Edwin A. Bock, Robert D. Calkins, Robert B. Highsaw, John C. Honey, F. P. Kilpatrick, James M. Mitchell, Coleman B. Ransone, and Silvan S. Tomkins.

I should like to thank Gene Anderson, Edith Pavey, and Caridad Alviar for making clean typescript of an almost undecipherable manuscript. Finally, I must acknowledge the patience and forbearance of my wife, Rosanna, and my daughter, Mary, who put up with me during many evenings, week ends, and holidays when these essays were in preparation.

Contents

1. *Is man a political animal?*

MAN IS THE STARTING POINT IN ANY DIS-
cussion of capacity to govern. To come to some
conclusion regarding the politically significant characteristics of man is such a logical necessity that it is almost
self-evident. Man is both the subject and the predicate
of the governing verb, and unless we have some idea of
man's nature how can we talk sensibly about forms of
government, constitutions, public opinion, policies, procedures, goals or values?

Starting this way, we are in good company. Most of
the political philosophers have had in mind a pretty
definite idea of man's nature. [1] One of the earliest in
our own cultural ancestry said a good many years ago
that "man is by nature a political animal. And he who
by nature and not by mere accident is without a state, is
either above humanity, or below it." [2] Aristotle came
to these conclusions even though he lived through the

[1] Thomas Hobbes is a good example. Part I of the *Leviathan* (New
York: E. P. Dutton and Co., Everyman's Library, reprinted 1931) is
entitled "Of Man" and contains sixteen chapters on this important
subject. Political scientists, however, tend to be interested chiefly in
Chapters 13-15, dealing with "the natural condition of mankind," con-
tracts, and the laws of nature.

[2] F. W. Coker, *Readings in Political Philosophy,* II Aristotle, Read-

disintegration of the Greek city-state system and the incorporation of Greece into the Macedonian Empire. Something must have been lacking, however, for when the theoretical model of the Greek political scientists was followed, as some historians think it was, in the colonial garrison cities of the Roman Empire, the stability and strength which the scheme was designed to produce were achieved only temporarily and at the cost of progressive loss of vitality and governing capacity. Cities constructed according to the Greek model did not grow, and they did not live.

Those political philosophers who have not made their view of man explicit have implied it by the kinds of political systems they have prescribed for man. A theory of government has to be based upon a theory of human nature, for government is an activity of man. It is the activity, of all activities, which in the twentieth century is perhaps most critical. It would not be stretching the point too far to say that governmentally, civilization is in a critical condition.

"Statesmen," and even the more lowly "politicians," necessarily have in mind models of man when they are devising, revising, or operating the machinery of the state. These models existed before modern psychology existed, and perhaps some in current use today have their modern origins in the eighteenth century. One of these certainly is the concept of the rational man. Adam Smith's economic man is best known. He is a veritable Paul Bunyan whose sturdy shoulders have sup-

---

ings from the *Politics*, "The Nature, End, and Origin of the State" (New York: Macmillan, 1923), p. 57.

ported the development of that vast body of doctrine which goes by the name "economics," and which is the rationale for our system of producing and distributing goods and services that was once called capitalism, but which is now coming to be referred to as a mixed economy. We are greatly indebted to Adam Smith's giant for the theoretical support he has given to creating the world's most productive economy.

Equally important to us is the less publicized figure of the political man, also a rationalist to the core, but with the added desire to govern himself through the machinery of representative government. He too is clad in knee breeches, and powders his hair. He is a stout old fashioned fellow who was much in mind when the American system of government was launched on its independent course. [3] But he is even more improbable today than the economic man.

It is a shock now to be told that these two "giants in the earth" never existed—that they are not only figments of the imagination but are contrary to fact. This conclusion is, today, widely accepted by academicians and also by those of us who get our information second hand (and are too busy to get acquainted directly with the work of Adam Smith and the political reformers of the eighteenth century). Before accepting the idea that the eighteenth century statesmen were simply stupid and their models of man completely false, however, I should like to suggest a small point in their defense. It may be that these men were fully as sophisticated in

[3] It is hard to read the Declaration of Independence without gaining confidence in the judicious rationality of political man.

their comprehension of human nature as we are. Can we say that there were not within the ranks of mankind any physical counterparts for their models? I do not think so. And if the eighteenth century reformers in idealizing and slightly exaggerating these types were attempting to establish a model for general guidance as well as for analysis, have we any basis for assuming intellectual superiority? Again I do not think so. Their models have served us well, and while they no longer stand on pedestals of shining marble, I propose that we hold off a bit before we run them through the rock crusher to destroy them forever.

This point made, it must also be said that a great deal has happened since the momentous year 1776 when Adam Smith published his *Wealth of Nations* in London, and the "signers" put their names to the Declaration of Independence in Philadelphia. Empires have passed away to be succeeded by satellite systems; new nations have risen, and new economies have been created. A seventh continent has been added to the six and a global disorder is teetering on the brink of chaos, we are told, as it struggles to become a world order. The growth of knowledge in the past century is even more impressive. Universal education has become a general ideal in the United States and its appeal is spreading. The furtherance of knowledge has become a full-time occupation for tens of thousands of the best minds in America, and also in other continents. Not the least of these scholars are social scientists who have added greatly to knowledge of mankind.

Modern psychology, which is less than a hundred

years old, has produced a prodigious amount of data about man and many suggestive lines of theory which have opened new windows of understanding—I was about to say into man's soul. But that would not be an appropriate way to put it, for almost the first feat of the European experimentalists was to remove the concept of soul. The nineteenth century pioneers taking their running start from physiology, and freshly committed to scientific rigor, had no place for such a quaint archaism in the laboratory. No doubt this removal was necessary; for the soul as a concept was the captive of scholars in other fields, and it had come to have very restricted freedom of movement.

The modern laboratory approach to the nature of man, although it started in Germany, seems to have been most congenial to psychologists in America, where it has reached its peak and where it is said to be dominant in American psychology. Experimental psychology, animal psychology, environmentalism, behaviorism, and stimulus-response psychology (usually abbreviated to S-R) are familiar labels for the numerous groups of scientists in the goodly company of American psychologists. [4] What they have added to the knowledge of man is most important. No one can follow the trails these men have blazed without being impressed with their very great discoveries.

The scientific "drive" of the nineteenth century, to borrow a psychologist's term, also gave rise to another

[4] There were in 1958 approximately 17,500 professed or practicing psychologists in the United States, assuming that the membership of the American Psychological Association is a guide.

quite different approach to man. Starting in the medical clinic among persons no less devoted to rigorously scientific ideals, psychoanalysis proceeded along a parallel but entirely independent course to advance the knowledge of man. Who that is alive in the midtwentieth century can say that this body of doctrine and data has not had a profound impact upon the world of affairs as well as the world of knowledge? Whether we understand what the psychoanalysts have done or not, laymen have borrowed their terms and vulgarized their concepts: ego, id, extrovert-introvert, complex, repression, fixation, regression, and others. The *lapsus animi* and the *lapsus linguae* of my childhood have become the Freudian error of today, no longer meaningless mistakes.

Building on the work of the pioneers, successive generations of scientists have carried forward the research, elaborating, refining, and enriching doctrines. Sociologists and anthropologists similarly have made notable contributions to the knowledge of man. Merely to classify in broad categories the distinguishable fields of data and theory, and the schools of thought within them would be a prodigious exercise in itself—but an exercise that, fortunately, is unnecessary to make the point that we now have a rich body of material to which students of government can turn in getting a better understanding of man, the elemental stuff of politics. One can not attend seriously to the teaching of the learned men in even one of these sub-categories of broad fields without being enormously impressed by the value of the information available and the insight which it permits.

There is a difficulty, however, in this situation.

Although data are abundant and increasing, and the body of theory about personality is expanding, the experts do not agree in their conclusions about man. Theories not only differ but conflict. Familiarity with the doctrines of one school seems to bring insight, but a second raises doubts, and a third turns doubt into confusion. Authors of a leading text on personality theory urge young psychologists to be "true believers," to accept with enthusiasm one set of doctrines, any one, and to concentrate their research in testing their chosen theory.[5] It is too early, they think, to attempt a synthesis.

They have a number of reasons for offering this advice. Some theories lack sufficient "formal clarity." Some theories not only differ but are in "flat disagreement" with others. And there are some which "are a long way from possessing demonstrated empirical utility." [6] To put it more bluntly, the judgment of the experts on the experts is that in their conclusions about human personality, there is at present much that is confusing, conflicting, and irrelevant. There are persuasive hypotheses about man's nature, but no real explanation of his *being* that is both comprehensive and universal.

There is a further difficulty that the data are most nearly adequate, and the theoretical certainty greatest concerning the smallest points.[7] A large part of the

[5] Calvin S. Hall and Gardner Lindzey, *Theories of Personality* (New York: Wiley, 1957), p. 556.

[6] *Ibid.,* p. 554 ff.

[7] This is an old complaint. "Much of the academic psychology, in its quest for precision and prestige, has quit studying the problem with

research effort has gone into studying bits and pieces of human behavior. Man has been taken apart and studied in a knocked-down state. Very small segments of behavior have been examined in detail, not total behavior. This emphasis has been particularly characteristic of American psychology. Leadership in the effort to put man back together again may be credited largely to the influence of psychiatrists, psychoanalysts, and clinical psychologists who deal with problems of whole men even though they be disturbed men. The currently increasing efforts to develop theories of personality are encouraging, although this is far from a general movement in psychology. But the experts are not yet ready to come to agreement.

In this situation, what should we do? Wait for another hundred years of research? Another century of debate? Would there be agreement then on a comprehensive theory of man? It may be doubted. Obviously neither the layman nor the psychologist (as a human being) can wait. He has to act on what he knows although it is inadequate. In day-to-day decisions he has to make assumptions about his fellow man, and he has to go ahead.

It would be disingenuous to pretend that we do not have other resources to draw upon than modern psy-

---

which it is ostensibly engaged, and has substituted a minor field of physiology therefore. In so doing, it has lost any criterion for testing the relevance of the results of particular researches for the understanding of personality because it has no master concepts of personality." Harold D. Lasswell, *Psychopathology and Politics* (Chicago: University of Chicago Press, 1930), p. 15.

chology and the behavioral sciences. There is direct experience which offers new lessons each day on the nature of man. A great part of humanistic learning is concerned with man's nature, and who will say that its insights are not very great? In turning to scientific research, to psychology, to the "behavioral" scientists generally to see what they have discovered, we are not discrediting the traditional lore which civilization has accumulated. Rather we are looking for a sifting of conflicting concepts that have been inherited, for verification or disproof, for refinements and extensions, for greater insights, and deeper penetrations, for explanations of how as well as why, for significant generalizations to go beyond simple case-by-case treatment of man. Recognizing that it is not within our grasp to know fully the nature of man, we are still justified in seeking to discover what new has been added to ordered knowledge. Having noted the difficulties, the disagreements, and the limitations, we must also conclude that there is much to be learned.

Fortunately our task is less difficult than that of the personality theorist. We are here concerned only with those characteristics of man which are politically significant. As we sort over the findings of the past century, attempting to identify data and interpretations on which there is substantial agreement, what do we discover that has a bearing on man's capacity to govern? [8]

[8] I shall try to present only those points on which there is substantial agreement. I am not making new points; but am noting points which have been made persuasively by psychologists (broadly defined) and which have been more or less accepted.

1. One politically significant discovery is man's *multiplicity*. He is not a single system, but a combination of systems. This was where the eighteenth century models of the economic and political man were misleading. They implied that man is solely and consistently rational at least in economic and political matters, and they implied that different men are equally rational. Although we are far from clear or agreed as to the nature of the systems of energy, motivation, learning, decision, and expression which operate in man, it is clear that there are a number of interacting systems. We are indebted to the psychoanalysts for leadership in making this point so persuasively. When the laboratory men had disposed of the body-mind-soul trilogy, to get on with their research, the clinical men created a new trilogy of id, ego, and superego to get on with their diagnoses. [9]

Freud's voyage of discovery into the unconscious mind proved it was there and opened up a new psychic continent to exploration. His development of the free fantasy interview was also a northwest passage that made exploration possible, although it can not carry a very large volume of traffic. [10] Jung went beyond Freud's

[9] Some eight different theories of the ego are in use, each employed by an appreciable body of experts. Gordon W. Allport, "The Ego in Contemporary Psychology," *Psychological Review,* Vol. 50, 1943, p. 451 ff.

[10] Ernest Havemann has estimated that there are only 1,400 psychoanalysts in the world, that they could be treating not more than 14,000 patients, and that in all not more than 100,000 people have run the full course of psychoanalysis. *The Age of Psychology* (New York: Simon and Schuster, 1957), p. 64. This is hardly a mass therapy. The chief product of psychoanalysis has been not therapy, but ideas.

conscious, preconscious, and unconscious, and found
(he thought) a collective unconscious, as well as a
personal unconscious, with numerous archetype components: for example, the persona, the anima, and
animus, the shadow, and eventually the self. [11] I do
not begin to understand this process of analysis, but it
is clear that it has utility to clinicians in grappling with
very perplexing problems and it aids in getting to the
root of difficulties. It seems equally clear to the lay
observer that these somewhat personified concepts are
in function strangely like the soul which they displaced.
These postulated components are functionally alike in
serving the psychologist or psychotherapist on one hand
and the theologian on the other to explain qualities of
man's nature that are beyond simple description. Meta-
phorical figures are necessary to convey the ideas. The
psychologists and theologians are together also in using
the components to explain qualities in man which distinguish him from all other living creatures.

[11] Some subsequent psychoanalytic leaders have revised or trimmed
down this personality pantheon. But it is by no means obsolete.

Although Dr. Carl Jung has not attained a wide following and his
influence seems to be declining, one of his concepts is to me very
helpful in penetrating what is otherwise a great mystery. This is the
concept of the *anima* and *animus*. The *anima,* it appears, is the softer,
gentler, more feminine side of a man's unconscious; and the *animus* is
the tougher, more aggressive, and more masculine side of a woman's
unconscious mind. Until I came across this idea, I never could understand how it happened that when a sweet, gentle, little woman got
into an automobile with her husband at the wheel, she became immediately a sea captain governing her ship with an iron hand and
demanding instant obedience from the helmsman. Apparently the
smell of gasoline and the sound of the starter bring the *animus* in-
stantly to life.

2. A second psychological discovery which has political significance is the *interplay* among the constituent systems in man. He may operate on a highly rational level. The conscious mind then seems to function at its expected traditional best. Man is very reasonable, very rational, we say. But the unconscious may intervene subtly through the defense mechanisms of the ego and almost unperceptibly it may skew the conscious mind away from its rational approach to objective reality. On occasion also a more elemental action system may take control completely. Even our traditional language reflects this fact. For example, we say that man is in a "fit of anger," that he is "beside himself" with rage, or more simply that he is "mad." The popular terms are not entirely inaccurate. When sufficiently angered man is irrational and mad. The significance of the interacting systems is that man is capable of great rationality and great irrationality. The extremes are remarkable. Men compose judicial tribunals and also rioting mobs. They are capable both of severe logic and violence more savage than the beasts.

Man can be appealed to on many levels, and he can react on many levels. The appeal can be entirely reasonable, it can be a mixture of logic and subtle stimulus to inner anxieties, or it can be a direct challenge to the prehuman forces which lie latent but alive in the unconscious. This quality of man is both wonderful and terrible.

It is the discovery of the unconscious that has toppled the eighteenth century models of man from their pedestals. The sociologists and anthropologists, however, have confirmed the downfall by exposing the deep stream of nonrational behavior in which man floats on the current of convention which may be rationally functional or which may not be.

It seems clear to us today that the rational system in man was stressed too exclusively by political theory in the past. It was assumed to be too rigid and complete; and so man's nature was misconceived and misrepresented. But should we not ask ourselves today whether the contemporary popular emphasis upon man's nonrational and irrational systems is not an equally gross exaggeration? [12] And are not the consequences even more disturbing? If the Madison Avenue approach to man, whether in making sales or seeking votes, starting with the idea that the basis of man's motivation is in his elemental impulses and anxieties, assumes that man's rational system can be compelled to act in a preferred way by massive stimulation of unconscious desire, or basic anxiety, what are the consequences? For example if international diplomacy becomes largely a matter of arousing fear in foreign countries, do we intimidate potential enemies or do we more certainly make ourselves neurotic?

Will the massive stimulation of anxiety push man steadily toward emotional instability? Or will the continued stress upon anxiety-stimuli unaccompanied by

[12] This vulgar exaggeration certainly is not Freudian in the literal sense, for Dr. Freud believed that bringing to the light of consciousness the unconscious origins of psychic difficulties was itself the best means of curing neurotic malady. His conviction that understanding and reason are the means of dealing with the consequences of unreason was central both to his theory and his therapy.

overt deleterious consequences, lead to "extinction" of the stimulus (to borrow an S-R term)? Will the massive assault on the unconscious and the elemental drown reason as an approach to objective reality? Or will man react so as to escape from the flood through his rational processes, striving to find relief from oppressive psychic pressures by understanding them and so gaining a measure of relief? Will the contemporary reliance on the irrational model of man depress man to its likeness, or will new confidence in man's rational capacity emerge? [13] To the extent that you are aware of your own reactions to modern advertising, to current campaigning, and to irrational propaganda, what do you find to be the trend in yourself? This would be a clue. [14]

Like the economic man and the political man of the eighteenth and early nineteenth centuries, the neurotic model in popular use today is a partial truth which as such caricatures reality. It, too, is inadequate. To in-

[13] It is desirable at this point to pass over these questions without attempting to answer them for two reasons. The first is that such an attempt would unduly interrupt what is intended to be a briefly suggestive identification of politically important characteristics of man. The second is the probability that there is no simple answer. The answer "depends." It depends upon some of the matters to be discussed subsequently, the society which men create, and the leadership which society produces.

[14] There is increasing evidence that many election campaigns have little effect upon voters' decisions. They seem to be little interested in what the candidates have to say, perhaps because it is "just campaign talk." The campaigner's reaction is, "They seem to have their minds made up." Perhaps inflation runs its course in public discussion as in finance, and words are discounted so much that they no longer have much "purchasing power."

corporate what is known, a new model will have to make allowance for interacting systems and for variable dominance among them.

3. This brings us to the third politically significant fact, documented, or at least elaborated, by social science research of the past century. It is man's *relation to his culture,* particularly his dependence on it. Man without a culture is only an abstraction, contrary to fact. Man could not have become man except in a society; and generation by generation he can only live, and grow, and find satisfaction in and through society. [15] For all of their past utilities we must admit that the contract theories of the origin of the state are completely fantastic. A "state of nature" is for man unnatural. Man could not imagine such a thing as a contract unless he lived in a society which had achieved some degree of advancement governmentally, and the society in which he has been reared is a part of him.

Although the consequences of cultural dependence are endlessly complex, the explanation is relatively simple. Man has little instinctive adjustment to life, perhaps none. He is the only living creature which does not. He is born in a completely dependent state which is prolonged. No inborn adjustment to the world emerges as he becomes physically mature. He has to

[15] Toynbee's view: "We have said that primitive societies are as old as the human race, but we should more properly have said that they are older. Social and institutional life of a kind is found among some of the higher mammals other than man, and it is clear that mankind could not have become human except in a social environment." Arnold J. Toynbee, *A Study of History,* Abridgment of Volumes I-VI, by D. C. Somervell (New York: Oxford University Press, 1947), p. 49.

learn it, painfully, the hard way. He has his natural needs and physiological drives, but to satisfy or fulfill them he must be guided by reason and rely on his effort. Man must live by the sweat of his brow forever, even though the cause may be anxiety rather than manual labor. In this respect all generations start even.

4. When we put alongside this characteristic a fourth point of political significance we begin to appreciate the complexities of man's existence. This is man's *uniqueness*. Now we are talking about the individual. "All of the animals in the world are psychologically less distinct from one another," says Allport, "than one man is from other men." [16] Man is inescapably an individual. "Nature's investment in individuality stands forth chiefly in *homo sapiens.*"

Man can neither escape from himself nor from his culture. He is born into a group, is molded by it, and finds his life satisfactions in it. Yet he also is a unique individual who has to give effect to his individuality through his affiliations with his social context. This double necessity demands a nicely discriminating course of action by man as an individual and by men as a group. Man must conform, but for his highest development and fullest satisfaction, he must conform to the group in such a way as to express, not suppress, his

---

[16] Gordon W. Allport, *Becoming: Basic Considerations for a Psychology of Personality* (New Haven: Yale University Press, 1955), p. 23.

Hobbes seems to have begun his chapter on the "Natural Condition of Mankind" with the antithetical assumption that differences can be disregarded and that men are alike or "equal." See his opening paragraph, *Leviathan,* Chap. 13.

uniqueness. He must establish his own best style of life amidst the general ways of living. Similarly if the group is to reach its full potential public policy and group expectations must insist on sufficient conformity to permit the group to function but not so much as to hinder individual fulfillment and progress. So we have for every man a dilemma to be faced, and a balance to be sought—a problem that he solves from day to day more or less satisfactorily in terms of his genes, his history, and his situation. And for society we have an overall problem of general public policy to be solved in terms of the society's degree of advancement. It must have order, but no order is stable without progress. And how is progress possible without individual deviations from the norm?

5. The fifth feature of considerable political significance is a fortunate companion of the third and fourth. It is man's *versatility,* or adaptability. This has been documented for us by both the behaviorists in psychology and the students of group behavior in anthropology and sociology. Watson argued that all tastes are learned and that they might have been learned differently. Not every one will go that far, but it is clear that men do learn to live happily in radically different physical circumstances: in the arctic and the tropics, on mountains and in deserts, in isolated homesteads and in metropolitan cities. [17] To do so they have developed cultures

---

[17] Erich Fromm's statement is dramatic. "It is true indeed, that man, in contrast to the animal, shows an almost infinite malleability; just as he can eat almost anything, live under practically any climate and adjust himself to it, there is hardly any psychic condition that he can-

with differences which go far beyond the physical diversities of the Earth's surface, and which are an expression of the unique preferences of the individual members of the generations that have produced these cultural atolls. Man has proved that he can live anywhere on Earth and he has created cultures which in their variety suggest infinity.

6. A sixth facet closely related to the fifth is growth. That is, versatility has a dimension in time. Men not only have different capacities in differing degrees; but they change. They have the capacity to grow in knowledge, understanding and interests, to develop new tastes, new affiliations, and new skills. The unfolding of inborn capacities in meeting the challenge of new circumstances and in responding to new ideas can be a lifelong process, giving great satisfaction day by day and year after year.

It takes nearly twenty-five years for the new-born infant to reach physical maturity. During this time he also is laboring more or less vigorously to develop his capacities and skills for satisfactory participation in his society's way of living. The attitude and habit of growth may be established in this process. But nature nevertheless continues the experience. Passing from

---

not endure, and under which he cannot carry on. He can live free and as a slave, rich and in luxury, and under conditions of half starvation. He can live as a warrior, and peaceably; as an exploiter and robber, and as a member of a co-operating and loving fellowship. There is hardly a psychic state in which man cannot live, and hardly anything which cannot be done with him, and for which he cannot be used." *The Sane Society* (New York: Rinehart, 1955), p. 18.

the parental family to one's own family is like moving
from elementary school to the university. Lessons are
more vivid and illuminating as well as more demanding.
Normally the process of beneficial development continues and is intensified. Our society also makes
possible an extended period of growth for men in many
vocations, and these are some of the most satisfying
vocations—also the most demanding. Whether growth
is merely a habit established by nature and deepened
by the peculiarities of our culture, or is a product of
deep-seated inborn characteristics we need not try to
determine here. Neither need we assume that the characteristic of continuing development is equally strong
in all men. Presumably the characteristic varies in intensity, rate, and range. But it is here about us in the
people of our own culture, and is most obvious among
those for whom the culture has already provided optimum conditions for individual development. It is a
characteristic that feeds on itself.

Allport has developed the characteristic of growth
most skillfully in his treatment of personality as a lifelong process of becoming something not inborn, not
even formed in early life but a personal and purposeful
creation that does not approach full development
without a long and continued effort. [18] Inherited "in-
tentional characteristics" are important, but they only
start and steer the process of growth. Infancy also is
important. In this he agrees with the Freudians. But
he differs by doubting that infantile experiences do

[18] Allport, *Becoming: Basic Considerations for a Psychology of Personality,* especially Chap. 20, p. 88 ff.

more than determine whether the individual shall have normal freedom for continued growth. If there has not been a psychologically crippling infancy, he believes that the individual's "primary modes of addressing himself to the future" will prevail and that he will be free to grow toward his own goals and values, and to some degree achieve fulfillment in his own unique personality.

7. Finally, a seventh politically significant characteristic is man's need and capacity for *affection*. For normal development the infant requires the warmth of affection as well as the warmth of physical protection. Without it, full development is arrested and severe limits are set to later natural development. At some stage later the child must, for his own good, develop an outgoing affection for his peers. The exploitive love of child for mother is not enough, he must give as well as receive on a basis of equality. As the youth moves into adult life the need to love and be loved is no less fundamental, but perhaps more subtle and urgent.

Fromm has said "The necessity to unite with other human beings, to be related to them is an imperative need on the fulfillment of which man's sanity depends. This need is behind all phenomena which constitute the whole gamut of intimate human relations, of all passions which are called love in the broadest sense of the word." [19] The oneness with his fellows which the individual craves can be achieved only in this way. For the unity achieved by domination or submission destroys the individual as it absorbs him.

[19] Fromm, p. 36.

The sociologists working independently have confirmed the fact of man's affinity for affection. The famous Hawthorne experiment of twenty-five years ago disclosed in detail how inevitable it is for people to envelop an organization designed for formal functions, with a network of warm human relations, in which they can find emotional satisfaction. [20] It demonstrated also that personal relations which are fully satisfying in a working group can give a terrific lift to morale and productivity, as by-products. Without ties of affection to his fellows, man is alone and incomplete.

In our reckless effort to harvest some of the fruits of scientific inquiry, we have identified seven characteristics of men and women in our culture (western civilization)—we would not go beyond—which seem to have significance for our consideration of America's capacity to govern. These are (giving them short labels):

1. Multiplicity—a system of systems, not a single system.
2. Interplay—systems interact, even compete.
3. Cultural dependence—culture molded, and culture bound, but not rigidly.
4. Uniqueness—his most distinguishing feature; in our advanced society, practically infinite.
5. Versatility—within the race great capacity to adapt.
6. Growth—in free men of western civilization it is ideally a lifelong process.
7. Affection—at all stages man needs to give and receive it.

[20] Perhaps the best interpretation of these experiments is still Elton Mayo's *Human Problems of an Industrial Civilization* (New York: Macmillan, 1933).

These are certainly not all of the points that might be made. The survey could go on endlessly and more expertly! But for our purposes they will suffice. Before moving to consider their implications, however, we may remind ourselves of the danger of over-stressing any one characteristic or of carrying it too far. This is the easiest way to go astray in our views. The multiplicity of systems within man and their interplay tend to make for restraint in the observer as well as unpredictability in the actor. We need to be very discriminating in applying any set of generalized ideas about man to particular men in specific situations. John Dewey has said that despite all that is known about man and education, it is not possible to predict how any single individual will react to an educational experience. What it will do to him and what he will do in consequence we do not know. University professors who have had long experience have seen the unexpected and unpredictable happen so often even within the conventional influences of the university that they accept this as a truism. Parents who see their sons and daughters leave home for the university have some perhaps inarticulate misgivings, not just because of the bills, but because they are now relatively powerless to affect the course of development. They can only realize, and accept it reluctantly, that the son or daughter to achieve his own development must get out of the nest, and free himself from home influences—except those which already have become a part of himself.

With this preliminary word of caution, I should like to put two questions.

1. In the light of what we know about the nature of man, is democratic self-government a viable institution? That is, are men's characteristics such that they can govern democratically and successfully on a continuing basis? Or is political democracy destined to be a passing phase in a trial and error process of political evolution? An alternative possibility is that democracy is at best a disguise to gain acceptance for what is actually concentrated power. What do you think?

2. Is the kind of democratic society in which we live the "good society"? That is, does it accommodate the needs of man, or does it defeat and frustrate him?

2. *Is democracy viable?*

THE VIABILITY OF DEMOCRATIC SELF-GOVernment is a matter of concern to many thoughtful people in democratic societies today. They have seen apparently democratic governments disintegrate under pressure; and they can observe signs of disruptive internal pressure in their own democratic systems. Many devoted democrats fear for the future of democracy. What have the scholars learned about society that bears on the survival and development of democracy?

A good bit has been learned about societies by sociologists and anthropologists over the years. Important distinctions between primitive and advanced societies have been made, and some peculiarities of American society have been identified, at least tentatively.

Origins are a logical starting point. It is now clear that man and society have always been together. Man never lived in a "state of nature"; for society of some sort is his natural state, although it is a state which his progenitors have created, and which he modifies.

The sociologists are also convinced, and I believe them, that society and government have always been together. There are no apolitical societies. "Government is one aspect of society . . . a phenomenon that emerges within social life, inherent in the nature of social order. . . . Wherever man lives on the Earth, at whatever level of existence, there is a social order, and always permeating it is a government of some sort." [1]

Common Elements

Taking a look at societies without too much advice of counsel (from the behavioral scientists), we note that there are four elements common to all kinds and varieties:

(1) One is authority—force plus an acceptance, that, within limits, which vary with the society, creates within the members of the state a sense of its rightfulness. All political theories have had something to say about power and its role. Some have made it the dominant element in politics.

(2) A second element is functional utility. All societies are in the nature of mutual benefit associations in which men provide each other with goods and services, order, and associational satisfactions. Societies may vary in their efficiency in providing mutual benefits, and obsolescence is a factor, but they are service associations.

(3) All have some procedures for joint or collective action on the part of the entire society—a third element. There is some machinery of state and some over-all corporate character in all societies.

[1] Robert M. MacIver, *The Web of Government* (New York: Macmillan, 1947), p. 21.

(4) The fourth element has been somewhat overlooked, or at least understressed, by some political
theorists in our recent past. It is the obligation of
members to serve, contribute, or even sacrifice for society. Many individual services or contributions are a
matter of convention or propriety; but for some there
are sanctions.

Civilizations

Advanced societies differ in important respects from
primitive societies. They are not only larger and
longer lived, but, more significantly, they change. They
are dynamic in contrast to the static primitive society.
Toynbee has developed the thesis that primitive societies which are confronted with a challenging condition
become civilizations when they react successfully to the
challenge, and in doing so change themselves in such a
way that they develop the capacity to keep on growing. [2]
The element which distinguishes a civilization from
other societies is progress.

A second difference is the existence of procedures for
determining social goals and for effecting change. Not
all change is controlled or sanctioned, but at important
points there tends to be political action to stimulate,
guide, control, or defend progressive change. The state
acquires the function of encouraging or promoting
progress as well as the function of maintaining order,

[2] Arnold J. Toynbee, *A Study of History*, Vols. 1-3 (London: Oxford
University Press, 2nd ed., 1935). The short statement of Toynbee's
thesis is to be found in the abridgement by D. C. Somervell, Chaps.
IV-XII (New York: Oxford University Press, 1947).

and so acquires a dilemma which simpler peoples escape. The dilemma of order versus progress is one of the prices of civilization. The machinery and procedures of change also involve conscious and deliberate decisions, a consciousness of corporate life and purpose that is not unlike the growing child's increasing awareness of himself and eventually of his mission in life.

A third difference is an increasing specialization in the contributions and role of individual members. This specialization permeates the political processes as well as other phases of advanced societies.

Democracy

When an advanced society begins to take on democratic features, still further differences appear which add to its effectiveness, and which also create problems. What are these distinguishing characteristics of democracy as we know it? Without any intent to be definitive, I suggest four elements. One is a tendency toward general participation in the process of determining goals and in the procedures, especially the political procedures, of joint action. In a democracy the ultimate ratification of decisions on policy and the choice of the political leaders in charge goes to an electorate which if not universal is at least highly representative.

The second is increasing awareness of and deference to the individual and widening distribution throughout society of political, economic, and social benefits.

The third is the development of a more complex

substructure within society, which is not monolithic or
even feudal in nature. We commonly refer to this as a
pluralistic characteristic of democratic society. People
are not isolated citizens within the state. They are
members of families, members of formal business, social,
and religious organizations. They constitute even more
significant informal organizations within and cutting
across formal organizations. They identify themselves
with cliques, classes, and movements; and they have
some choice as to the nature and extent of their participation. The individual citizen is a concept, but hardly
a reality. He always acts with reference to his fellows
and his affiliations, almost never alone. [3]

To a very considerable extent, also, the substructures
are "voluntary associations" which perform functions
that are socially useful, even essential. We are so
familiar in the United States with a host of nongovernmental organizations which perform religious, educational, cultural, welfare, and civic functions that we
take them for granted. These functions may be "privately" initiated and established; and some of them may
be passed on to government eventually. The voluntary associations, in the latter case, then may become
interest groups to see that governmental action carries
on, and to shape and influence governmental decisions.
There are always new voluntary associations to take the
place of those which lapse or languish. Religion is in

[3] This is one of the conclusions drawn from an intensive study of
voting behavior. See Bernard R. Berelson, Paul F. Lazarsfeld, and
William N. McPhee, *Voting, A Study of Opinion Formation in a Presidential Campaign* (Chicago: University of Chicago Press, 1954), p. 507.

the hands of voluntary associations. So are many welfare functions, even in the welfare state. The arts in important realms depend on the patronage of civic, philanthropic, and other "private" organizations. "Reforms," which are an important aspect of "politics," characteristically first come on the scene as "movements" set in motion by a few individuals and carried well on the road to public acceptance by voluntary associations.

The economy similarly may be regarded largely as a system of interacting voluntary organizations. The open market, which has not entirely vanished, is perhaps a striking example of dependence upon horizontal adjustments of only loosely "controlled" individuals and organizations for vital economic decisions. Despite the disputes, the friction, and the conflicts which dramatically attract attention, it is the smoothness of the economic machine's operation that is most impressive. Without arguing for either more or less central control, and without attempting to favor or oppose industrial concentration, it is still possible to make the point that initiative and discretion on vital matters are widely scattered, and that a large number of decisions which are of basic importance to society are left to horizontal adjustments between groups and individuals.

The voluntary associations themselves, whether economic or civic, are the product of individual initiative; and the distinguishing characteristic of a democratic society is its ability to produce individuals who can and do organize joint action upon new problems and to perform new and important social functions. The capacity for spontaneous creation of new substructures is more significant than the mere existence of the resultant pluralism in a democratic society. The existence of this power to generate and to operate associations for special purposes, relying not on force but on the subtler sanctions, is the fourth mark of an advancing democratic society.

It is obvious that the characteristics of a democratic society create problems at the same time that they may add to effectiveness. General participation may be at the risk of folly. Deference to the individual may endanger the common welfare. Pluralism can bring costly conflict as well as more satisfying social organization. Dependence on voluntary associations to meet new needs and perform socially important functions may lead to error and disaster as well as ready adaptability and high productivity. These hazards make it appropriate to consider certain prerequisites to the success of political democracy which the sociologists have discovered. Their judgment is not final, of course, but it is persuasive.

Democratic Prerequisites and Difficulties

The first prerequisite of democratic government is "a sufficiently general standard of technical skill and literacy." [4] Some go farther and argue that the technical skills must include considerable capacity for

---

[4] Elton Mayo, *The Social Problems of an Industrial Civilization* (New York: Macmillan, 1945), p. xii.

abstract thought in reading, and writing, and speaking.[5]

A second prerequisite is "a sufficiently high standard of living throughout . . . society" to remove, or at least limit, the factor of hunger from politics and to moderate the effects of differences in wealth. [6] If the general standard of living is high, differences above the general level tend to have less political significance. An illustration of this factor no doubt was the revival of democratic vitality in Western Europe following a substantial improvement in productivity and living standards.

A third requisite is sufficient homogeneity to produce reasonable agreement on questions which are generally felt to be important. [7] People must have reasonably similar moral values. There must be enough agreement over a wide enough range of matters so that in critical decisions rational processes do not break down.

A fourth requisite is reasonable stability within the social and economic order. Things must not change too much, too fast. An advanced society lives by progress, but an attempt to go too fast tends to destroy the emotional security which is an essential basis for a rational approach to public affairs. [8]

[5] Chester I. Barnard, *Organization and Management: Selected Papers* (Cambridge: Harvard University Press, 1948), p. 49.

[6] Mayo, p. xii.

[7] See the discussion of this requisite by Chester I. Barnard, p. 48.

[8] Berelson, Lazarsfeld, and McPhee (p. 313) conclude that "The intensity of conflict must be limited, the rate of change must be restrained, stability in the social and economic structure must be main-

The conduct of government in a democratic society also presents some difficulties which distinguish it from simple societies, and from advanced societies which are not democratic. First of all is the difficulty of harmonizing the advanced society's trend toward increasing specialization of function and the democratic society's need for more general participation in its governing process. An undiscriminating approach to it makes of this difficulty an inescapable dilemma. Inability to develop representative institutions crippled the ancient Greeks. The town meeting democracy of eighteenth century rural New England was fine in its day, but it is not a model that can be followed generally in twentieth century America.

As advanced democracies have discovered, however, the forces of specialization and participation do not constitute a true dilemma. There is a three-part solution which now has been well tested. One part is representative government. A second is delegation to the executive of authority to decide many questions. These include emergency questions, technical questions, and repetitive questions. (The last two of these categories account for the great growth of administrative

---

tained, a pluralistic social organization must exist, and a basic consensus must bind together the contending parties." The study of history apparently teaches the same lesson as the study of Elmira. Toynbee concludes that no society can leap to Utopia or turn the clock back to the good old days. The effort to bring off either feat, which is characteristic of "disintegrations of civilizations," leads to disaster of various sorts. See his discussion of "Archaism," and "Futurism," *The Study of History* (London: Oxford University Press, 1939, 1955), Vol. 6.

discretion in modern democracies.) The third part of
the solution, a consequence of the first two parts, is that
only the broadest questions and the ultimate choices
need be submitted to the electorate. This restraint in
calling electors to the polls can increase the importance
and the effectiveness of the electoral process. Annual
elections and the long ballot seem to be obsolete in the
complex conditions of an advanced democratic state as
we know it today.

A second difficulty of democratic government in an
advanced society is more subtle; and no fully satisfactory answer has yet been found. This is the
psychological disturbance caused by social change. Economic progress has its social cost. Man, without an
inborn way of life, sets great store by the way of living
which he learns and to which he is accustomed.
Familiar ways, familiar customs, and familiar situations
give a sense of security that is seriously disturbed if
social change is rapid. There is an optimum rate of
change, but it is not easy to find it. Changing
industrial technology, rural-urban migrations, and
inter-regional movements all tend to weaken the individual's sense of security, and to reduce, at least
temporarily, the associational satisfaction which he derives from everyday living. The consequent irritation
and anxiety have their political consequences. As the
social disturbance increases, man tends to become less
dependable in his rationality.

In addition, there are operational difficulties more
or less inherent in democratic government, which are
not insurmountable, but which become serious if the

public is politically unsophisticated, if the organic structure and policies of government are ill designed, or if the leadership is weak. On this subject Barnard has argued that many decisions of public policy have to be made in abstract terms which seem to be accepted, but which are not actually understood. [9] When they come to be applied concretely, and the significance is more apparent, people do not conform, although it seemed that they had intended to.

There is also a certain amount of delay in reaching a consensus upon which decisions can be based in the democratic process. This creates difficulty when the situation demands prompt action. Political debate as we know it also has some inherent limitations. It tends to stress reasons for action which people seldom agree on. It is much easier for them to agree on a program itself than upon their reasons for doing so. If the rational level is not very high, and if veracity is not a prime consideration, political discussion can create animosity rather than consensus. Barnard adds up all these points and sees that they place a real burden upon democratic leadership. [10] Wise and positive leadership can deal with these difficulties; but it takes energy and capacity. In other words, democracy demands more capable leadership, and probably considerably more of it, than does a nondemocratic society. Or so it seems.

Does this mean that it is less efficient? That question, of course, cannot be answered without considering also the products and benefits of democracy.

[9] Barnard, pp. 31-45.
[10] *Ibid.*, p. 42.

Man's Democratic Capabilities

Is man able over any considerable period of time to meet the requirements and deal with the problems which democracy presents? Is a democratic society consistent with his nature and within his capabilities? The general answer, I think, depends on five subsidiary questions:

1. Is man sufficiently co-operative?
2. Is he motivated? Does he want self-government?
3. Is man sufficiently rational?
4. Is there a natural basis in man for development of the concept of the public interest in any effective sense?
5. Are there enough men with enough good will to shoulder the responsibilities and make the necessary sacrifices?

Taking up these points one at a time, the first is easiest and most reassuring. The co-operation required is well within man's capacities. His associational impulses and satisfactions are in general more than adequate—although his individualistic tendencies are equally deep-seated. An accommodation of the two tendencies can be and is achieved in every culture. The cultural individualism which western civilization has fostered, in fact, has been accompanied by the creation of numerous partially independent and partially interacting groups in a complex pluralistic society such as that of the United States—a society that exceeds any other in the degree of co-operation required. Nowhere are the organizing capacity and the associational tendencies greater than the United States of America. The self-generating co-operating collectivism of pluralistic America makes the collectivism of Russia look very elementary indeed. On this point of co-operative capacity, democracy is well within man's limits.

On the question of motivation, i.e., desire for self-government, there are a number of points to be considered, some of them disquieting. First of all, there is no evidence anywhere of any general inborn desire to govern. The taste for governing is acquired. Some men do come to seek political power and to derive satisfaction from exercising it, and the governing process in an advanced society offers an outlet for many personality types. The sampling which has been done suggests that the number of psychic patterns found in modern government is great. But as yet we have no reliable data from which to conclude that there are fundamental differences in the combinations found in government and in business or other highly organized activities of society. Personality differences between governmental and nongovernmental employment may or may not be significant.

It is not even clear that there are significant measurable differences between democratic and nondemocratic governments in the combination of personality types that comprise the bulk of the governing personnel. At least superficially the bureaucracies of industrial states, democratic or nondemocratic, have many resemblances in size, function, and power. Democratic as well as undemocratic societies place much authority in the hands of public officials.

The important question for us at this point is not so

much the nature of officialdom as it is the nature of the rest of the population (and of the relations between the official and unofficial parts). In the nongoverning ranks is there enough desire to govern in a sufficient number of individuals scattered through society so that the work which democracy entails for the governed can be done? The double role of governing as well as being governed which democratic theory prescribes for the citizen is not realistic unless there is a significant number among the citizenry willing to perform the chores of democracy.

The question is whether there is sufficient interest in the generality of mankind and at high enough an intellectual level for the public to make rational decisions on the ultimate questions which it has to decide. In the United States, a world leader in nonvoting, this can be a disturbing question.

There is danger that at this point we may exaggerate the problem. We should remember that where the public is outspoken and has an active influence in the shaping of policy, the electorate only needs to ratify the controlling decisions on basic policies. Everything else can be delegated to *elected* representatives and *responsible* officials. What difference does it make if there is not avid general interest in elections at times when there are no important issues or choices to be made? In those times the delegation of authority to elected representatives and public officials is extended perfunctorily. The important fact is the public's ability to intervene *en masse* when there are important choices to be made, or when it is dissatisfied with the performance of responsible officials. This behavior is well within man's ability. We have all seen it done. [11] Democracy is not beyond man's capacity for essential participation. The capacity can be and is being cultivated successfully.

The question of the intellectual level of participation is more difficult. Obviously not many of us are capable of understanding the intricacies of all public problems and policies. Perhaps no one can comprehend them all, and some find it difficult to grasp any very firmly. Here again we must be on guard against exaggerating the difficulties. On no important subject do men make all of their decisions independently. We are members of families, groups, associations, and organizations. Within these various associations are people who have established themselves in our eyes as expert, wise, and responsible. We tend to be guided by their views. We want to hear what they have to say before making up our minds. We have learned from experience that their batting average in being right is very high. They tend to be opinion leaders. We also like to sample the reaction of our fellows. We respect the group's reaction. This can be dangerous if carried too far, or if the group is misled; but the tendency to go with our chosen group is also a force making for an eventual solid consensus.

The multiple memberships in separate but interlocking groups slow down the process of reaching a consensus, and require some double checking of preliminary conclusions. But in the long run the public's

[11] The 1959 recall election of Little Rock School Board members is perhaps an example. The desire not to be misgoverned rather than a positive desire to govern may be the basic motivation of democracy.

decision-making process is probably more rational because of its complex character. Again we come to the conclusion that men in the cultural pattern that we have in America can make sufficiently rational decisions to make democracy work. [12]

The key factor, obviously, is leadership. What kind of men play the leading roles within the substructures of a complex society as well as at the top of the governmental hierarchy?

The trend of education in Western society since the Renaissance has been to put increasing emphasis upon reason. There has been persistent effort to examine nature, man's experience, and man himself, objectively. There has been increasing concern with facts, and there have been notable efforts to perfect more rigorously exact and reliable ways of thinking about data. Man's

[12] Berelson, Lazarsfeld, and McPhee have concluded from their study of voting in one American city that people tend to vote with the group with which they identify themselves, but their vote is as much a matter of "taste" or "sense of fitness" as it is of choice on a high rational level. But in the aggregate they feel that the group is wiser than the individual voters. The fact that people differ in their interests and in the intensity of interests which they have, makes its easier for democracies to function. On any issue only a few people tend to feel very strongly; the rest go along. This makes it easier to get a decision on every issue. If everyone felt strongly on all issues, it might not be possible to get enough agreement to act. In this view, democracy depends upon the differential interest, and the corresponding differential apathy of the citizens. See *Voting*, Chap. 14, "Democratic Practice and Democratic Theory."

One wonders whether the authors of this valuable study would have come to just the same conclusions if they had studied relatively "hot" elections such as 1928 or 1952 rather than the lukewarm election of 1948.

subjective experience also has been brought within the realm which is subject to analysis in the effort to approach reality. The advancement of knowledge which has occurred in modern times is convincing evidence of Western civilization's success in emphasizing rationality. Although the impact of learning is by no means uniform, the rational emphasis has been sufficiently pervasive to affect increasing numbers of people positively. The effort to be "scientific" in fact has been observable on a wide front ranging from nuclear physics to business administration. An emphasis so important in an entire culture leaves few untouched, and must affect leaders of society most of all. There is no reason to minimize or to be discouraged about our assets on the rationality ledger. From the evidence we have, there is no reason to assume that democracy is beyond man's capacity for intelligent participation, measured in terms of both leadership and followership.

The fourth subsidiary question to be considered in reviewing the evidence as to whether man is in fact fit for democracy has to do with the public interest. Is there any psychological basis in human nature for the concept of the public interest—the critical standard in democratic government? That is, are we realistic to expect men to have a workable and generally understandable concept of the public interest? Unless members of the public, in making political decisions, as well as public officials in whom the public has to vest much discretionary authority, are able to identify the public interest as something distinguishable from their own interest, and unless they are able to give it

greater value than their own interest, effective and efficient government in a democracy is at best an accident,
a fortuitous creation of especially favorable circumstances, a creation which cannot endure.

The question is not whether man in a democracy is
capable of overriding loyalty to the public interest as
the public defines it. This question is easy. It is clear
that societies, particularly democratic societies, can
stimulate loyalty on an almost universal basis when the
public interest is sharply defined. The social scientists
have made it clear that this kind of loyalty is natural
in every society, and is a function of man's associational
needs and tendencies. [13]

Rather, the question is whether the individual man
can acquire dedication to the public interest as he, the
individual, defines it, and whether he can define it
honestly and realistically in such a way as to distinguish
it from his own interest when the two may diverge.
Inherent in the public interest is the idea of discretion,
individual discretion. It is a test both of faithfulness,
or loyalty, and of reason. It is an ideal which may call
upon the individual to do for the public what he sees
to be to the public's advantage, but which the public
may at the time not want. It calls for ability to be

---

[13] In his chapter on "The Politics of Prevention," Lasswell many
years ago wrote, "The excesses of heroism and abnegation are alike
primitive in their manifestations, and show that all the primitive
psychological structures are not antisocial but asocial, and may often
function on behalf of human solidarity." Harold D. Lasswell, *Psychopathology and Politics* (Chicago: University of Chicago Press, 1930),
p. 179.

rational and objective in this most discriminating judgment.

We are all aware of how easy it is to identify one's own interest with the public interest. Common knowledge of this very human tendency explains the laughter which greeted Secretary Wilson's famous remark that what is good for General Motors is good for the country.

But can the process in fact be turned 'round? Is it "natural" for men to identify their individual interests with the public interest? Although the psychological explanations of how it occurs vary, the psychologists agree that this is done naturally in normal, mature individuals. It is not freakish or exceptional behavior. It is a capacity within the reach of men generally. Whether it occurs "behavioristically" through a chain of associations starting with the conditioned reflex, is a matter of Freudian "identification and displacement," or is the result of "ego extension" leading to the development of a "generic conscience" in the mature adult we need not try to decide. [14] The scientists agree on the results. It is possible for man to envisage the public interest rationally, distinguishing it realistically from his own physical or financial welfare, and to give it an overriding loyalty.

The most striking and most general example of this phenomenon probably is the mother's identification of

[14] On this point, Allport's discussion of the growth of the mature personality through ego extension, propriate striving, and development of the generic conscience is illuminating and persuasive. Gordon W. Allport, *Becoming: Basic Considerations for a Psychology of Personality* (New Haven: Yale University Press, 1955), p. 44 ff.

her interest with the interest of her family—her children. She suffers if they suffer. She is anxious if anything indicates that all is not well with them. She enjoys their success. They are in a very real psychological sense a part of her "self." Human beings are capable of a similar identification in their relations with larger groups than the family, although it may not be so intense or so enduring. After rising above the point of satiety in meeting his physical needs, man normally identifies himself with a cause, an organization, or an enterprise, or he seeks wealth or power for its social significance. The enormous effort which democratic man expends in an advanced society is largely in pursuit of these symbolic goals. They are extensions of his "self," and he finds satisfaction in pouring out his energy upon them. In so general a process there is certainly no reason why man should not take the public interest as his own and devote himself to it in civic affairs, politics, and government. [15]

This inevitably becomes an intellectual process. He first has to envisage the public and in some way conceive of its interests. He identifies himself with this image. When this is done realistically it is the mark of a disciplined mind and a mature personality. It is a process

[15] Of course we are not arguing that a specific individual necessarily will formulate and adopt a rational view of the public interest in any given situation or that he necessarily will be faithful to this standard. If these were the facts, man would be less than man. He would be reduced to the ranks of other creatures with their instinctive compulsive adjustments. Our point is more limited—that an effective concept of the public interest is consistent with man's basic nature, and that it is a normal development in many men in Western society.

which is greatly aided by favorable circumstances, as we have already noted: a high general standard of living that lets people get beyond the compulsion of their direct hunger drive, sufficient homogeneity so that the determination as to the nature of the public interest is not too difficult, and some considerable (and perhaps habitual) ability to think abstractly and logically.

In this critical question, as with others, we must be on guard again against carrying an idea too far, and of so exaggerating the problem. The democratic ethic does not require the individual to subordinate himself to the group in all cases. There is a rule of reason, a point of discrimination, a working belief in the mutuality, or at least the reconcilability, of individual and public interests in most circumstances. For example, a soldier is not expected to throw away his life in every battle, or to endanger himself foolishly for inconsequential gains. He is trained to minimize danger and avoid risks so far as possible. A commander will yield ground to reduce loss of life in many circumstances. It is only armies with an insecure military tradition that encourages reckless bravery. But when the stakes are high, when the attainment of an objective is very important, then the soldier is expected, if necessary, to make the supreme sacrifice. [16]

16 The rationale of modern democracy with its legal protections to individual rights, and its limitations upon powers of government, is that the interests of the individual and the state, the authoritative agent of society, shall be reconciled on some reasonable basis, if possible. The state's overriding authority is recognized but restricted.

This brings us appropriately to the fifth question: Is there enough good will to move men to the extra effort, perhaps to sacrifice, when it may be needed? If our thesis is valid that it is not possible to operate any society without sacrifice, and that a democratic society relies more heavily than others upon voluntary effort and voluntary sacrifice, is this reliance unrealistic? Is man sufficiently capable of such behavior to permit democratic societies to count on it?

This is perhaps the most difficult question of all, and only a very general answer is possible. There are really two parts to the question. One part is possibility; the other is probability. As we have noted earlier, man must receive and must also give affection for his best development. It is clear that man is capable of great passion—love, hatred, anger. It is recognized also that his generally favorable or affectionate response to others varies greatly in its nature and intensity, ranging from the intense feeling of lovers, or of parents for children, to a very general good will or even apathy. Perhaps the basic question is whether there is sufficient latent good will among men generally that it will develop into compassion or concern when the need arises. And

---

The individual has legal rights and the state has legal power. The legal battles between the two have made the history of American constitutional interpretation an exciting story. What is not recognized, however, in a purely legal approach to the question is that any accommodation which results from either the individual's pushing his rights or the state's pushing its power as far as it can is likely to be arbitrary and unsatisfactory. A concept of the public interest calls for the exercise of discretion and perhaps restraint on the part of each party in going only so far as is necessary.

will the concern or compassion be great enough to move men to act?

Man has the potential for the good will essential to democratic survival and progress. But it has to be cultivated. It has to be cultivated in each child and in each generation. Although children, or adults, must differ in their capacities for affection, a healthy family environment in the pattern of Western Christendom is likely to get the child off to a good start. Public policy attempts to shield the child from psychologically crippling asperities through child labor laws, social security measures to aid dependent children, and much older regulations of morals. At the point when the child becomes conscious of problems of human relations, the Church attacks the question directly with complete and comprehensible doctrines of the fatherhood of God and the brotherhood of man. There are no more venerable nor well-tested doctrines in all western culture than these. But their impact must depend largely upon the warmth of the human context in which they are taught and received. The state makes its great contribution to the education of the child in human relations through the public school system. Here the effort has been to make it a place where reason, justice, and good will reign. When the teachers, in addition to technical competence, have genuine warmth and concern for their pupils, the school makes a tremendous contribution to the normal child's growth emotionally, as well as intellectually.

Are these measures enough to keep alive the essential spark of good will in democratic man? Or does the coldness of a vast and changing impersonal society freeze out man's capacity for affection and good will? We shall return to this question later.

Coming back now to the question with which we started, the viability of democracy, it would seem to me that belief in man's capacity to shoulder the burden of democracy successfully is justified. A democratic society is not inconsistent with man's nature, in so far as we know it. Democracy is viable.

Viable, but not certain. In fact, quite uncertain. Democratic governments have been short lived. The republics of Latin America for the most part have not yet attained the substance of democracy, although they have democratic aspirations, and have copied democratic forms. The democracies which came into existence after World War I had made the world safe for democracy have nearly all disappeared, most of them behind the iron curtain and some of them into the Soviet Union proper. Venerable France is now in a fifth Hollywood marriage with democracy; but will it last? All the Western world hopes so; but who can predict?

The new nation-states which followed World War II for the most part are not democracies, and the would-be democracies have had great difficulties. Most recently in Burma, Thailand, and Pakistan dictators have taken over the governing function—as is always the case, with the professed interests of the nation at heart.

There are apparently stable democracies in Switzerland, Scandinavia, the British Commonwealth, and in the United States. We have been an independent democratic state for 182 years, and we have had a more or less stable government under our present Constitution for 170 years. Britain has had a continuous government free of foreign intervention since the last successful invader took over in 1066, but the progress from feudalism to a democratic free society was a slow step-by-step process. Political power was highly concentrated as late as the early nineteenth century. If democracy is dated from the first electoral reforms of 1832, it is only a little over a century and a quarter old, although parliamentary government is, of course, much older. One could not make a very good statistical case for the survival of democracy on the basis of world experience. Democracy is not inconsistent with man's nature. But neither is it inherent in man's nature. Democracy is an achievement.

This brings us to the second broad question about democracy (with which we concluded our discussion of man as a "political animal"): Is the kind of democratic society in which we live the "good society"? That is, does it accommodate the needs of man, or does it defeat and frustrate him? If man is fit for democracy, is democracy fit for man?

The answer, it seems to me, turns on the extent to which a democratic society accommodates man's craving for both conformity and uniqueness, his desire for growth and self-fulfillment, and his need to give and receive affection. On the first of these points, man's need for both group membership and individuality, must we not conclude that a democratic society is better than an undemocratic society in meeting man's real needs? Compulsory uniformity is minimized. The maximum area is left to voluntary action. The pluralistic character of the democratic substructure offers wide choices in manner of conformity. Many combinations are possible in group affiliations, and one can be a "joiner" or not, as he desires. Freedom is by no means complete, but there is great freedom. No other society offers as much associational freedom as a democratic society.

On the second point, man's desire for growth, again democracy seems to be a good fit. Growth which is primarily satisfying is not possible without freedom and responsibility. Both of these challenges democracy offers. Choices are sometimes painful, and the costs of error are heavy. Responsibility is a burden, which at times may seem unbearable. To escape it, or at least reduce it, many of us try very hard, consciously or unconsciously, to keep some freedom of choice, but to avoid too many painful dilemmas. [17]

All of us at times may look back fondly to the happy days of childhood when loving parents carried the burden of responsibility, and ruled out most of the more dangerous choices. Without minimizing the pleasure of childhood for children, we must also recognize that the parental home can become a prison for the growing youth. Its screening of choices and its assumption of all important responsibility may actually prevent growth and individual development. The only way to become

---

[17] I tell my wife that the reason I got married was so that I would not have to select the menu for dinner. Although this is impressive evidence of confidence in her judgment, she does not seem to like this testimonial.

wise is to learn from experience, and the only way to become strong is to carry loads. Parents hope anxiously that children will have enough wit to learn something from the experience of others, and not make all of the old mistakes over again. A good many fathers, I am sure, have said to their sons in their university days, "Just because you are on your own, you are not compelled to be a dam' fool!" And there is much to be said for this dictum. But men do need the experience of making some mistakes for themselves to learn prudence—and to grow. Certainly there is no frustration more complete than that of the adult who has not been able to throw off the loving shackles of his father's home. Democracy does provide an opportunity for growth through individual choices, individual effort, and individual responsibility.

On the third point, man's need to give and receive affection, I am less sure. The democratic policy of spreading society's benefits widely seems to me to be the product of good will; but once this policy has been established and the benefits are systematized, do they cease to be in fact an expression of good will? Does the good will evaporate, or merely sink into the soil, from where it can well up later? Is there in democratic society also a consciousness of good will in others that kindles in one's self that same warmth toward others? Or is democracy an impersonal and cold society? It could be that in expecting everyone to assume the posture of a responsible adult, the member of a democratic society correspondingly takes a more impersonal posture toward his fellows.

We may ask ourselves, also, what is the effect of prosperity upon these tendencies? Does it increase or diminish this good will? A foreign public official recently traveling in the United States was greatly impressed by the friendliness of the people. It was amazing to him. But he was equally impressed by the wealth of the United States, and he was perhaps inclined to link the two, making wealth the cause of friendliness. We may accept the view that progress away from gross poverty increases democratic man's friendly tendencies. But is there a continuing relationship between increased wealth and increased good will? Or at some point in the increase of riches, does the friendliness and good will of democratic society fade away? What do you think?

Coming back now to the question which is the topic of our discussion—is democracy viable?—I believe we must answer that it is. The weight of evidence supports this view that man is fit for democracy and that democracy is good for man. But there is nothing inevitable about it. The achievement and continuance of a democratic society requires intelligent, sustained effort supported by and infused with good will.

At this point, I would like to put a question to prospective administrators. How would you measure capacity to govern in the United States? That is, capacity to preserve both our independence and our democracy? What are the factors on which you would base your estimate that we will or will not survive and progress as an independent democratic nation?

3. *How can capacity to govern be measured?*

THE SIMPLEST AND OLDEST TEST OF CAPAC-
ity to govern is survival, still a good test. But it has
limitations. Its chief definitive reading is negative, for
it does not measure degrees of success or differences of
capacity. Survival is an index which can be read only
in retrospect. It is a clock which tells what time it was
—never what time it is. The fact that a state has sur-
vived does not indicate that it will continue to. The
phrase "handwriting on the wall" is a reminder from
political and religious history that an empire apparently
at the peak of its wealth and power may already be
doomed. History seems to say that the powers that be
always have great difficulty in reading the handwriting.
With the aid of historical perspective we may also draw
the conclusion that wealth and military power are not
in themselves evidence of governing capacity.

The standard of progress would be better than the
simple test of survival, for this is very close to the essential vital principle of an advancing society. It would
also be possible to devise measures of progress that
would perhaps reflect differences in capacity. To use
such a standard, of course, it would be necessary to de-

fine progress, a task in itself. This should be done in some detail, and in concrete terms. We are less likely to get lost in the woods if we start with the concrete functions and problems of government.

A Concrete Problem-Solving Standard

Looking around us at our various levels and varieties of governments in the United States, considering the functions of these governments in our complex industrial order, and facing up to the problems which confront us as a nation, what is a concrete measure of governing capacity?

In terms of functions or problem-solving, there are four groups of problems which together are the test of capacity: First, there are certain normal or traditional functions which are integrated with the pattern of day-to-day living. For convenience we shall call them municipal functions. Second, there are the two great national imperatives, defense and "full employment." Third, there is the necessity, while carrying on these functions, of making sure that both individual freedom and individual loyalties to the country as a whole are maintained. Fourth, there is the task of contributing effectively to the healthy development of the larger Western Society of which we are a part.

The first category of municipal problems may be conveniently presented in three subdivisions: (1) law-and-order functions; (2) public-utility-type services; and (3) welfare-state activities.

The law-and-order functions range from suppression

of violence and fraud, through protection of the family as an institution, to defining and adjudicating property rights. These functions are basic in a civilized state, and they are more or less integrated with the vast body of customs, conventions, moral code, and institutional life which constitute the pattern of civilized behavior. They change, but not rapidly. We take law-and-order functions for granted, but that does not mean that they do not need to be well done. They are a basic foundation for everything else.

The public-utility-type services, the second subdivision, are indispensable to urban life and are the foundation of urban-industrial efficiency. We have to have highways (more and better highways), streets, mass transport, water, fire protection, recreational facilities, postal services, and above all, schools. They are essentials, and whether they are provided by public agents or by corporations affected with a public interest under public control, does not concern us here. They, also, are public essentials, which we have come to take for granted, but which contribute to the strength of American society in proportion to the standards of service and efficiency which they attain.

The welfare-state functions, in the third subdivision, are an outgrowth in more positive form of the ancient humane activities of society whose business it is to defend the individual man, woman, or child (often ultimately the child) against the accidents and destructive forces of an unpredictable nature and an imperfect society. Originally justified on humane grounds, their present more positive form is now seen to be a matter of social efficiency and of economic as well as psychic importance. The peculiar power of an advanced civilization lies in its advanced individual men and women whose fullest development must be fostered at all costs. The solidarity and psychic security which result from welfare-state functions well performed can be one of the effective guarantees of the nation's mental health and unity.

An interesting and revealing point to observe in the law-and-order category is the point at which change occurs. Here order and progress are accommodated. The ability to progress while maintaining order may be very close to the heart of capacity to govern an advanced society. Governmental regulation often may be the cutting edge of reform or progress in a society which seeks beneficial change—just as it may be the heel of reaction in a society which fears change and seeks to defend the *status quo* at all costs. New regulation in almost every field tends to be controversial, e.g., aeronautics, radio, T.V., atomic energy. Resistance to change, conflicts of interest, lack of consensus, uncertainties as to principle, and fallacious assumptions as to ambiguous facts are characteristics of new regulation which produce controversy. But if regulation succeeds, the line of movement is toward accommodation of interests, agreement on facts or at least stable positions with reference to them, and acceptance. Regulatory functions, like the others in the normal or traditional group increasingly are taken for granted as an essential component of American life.

All in this group of municipal functions have certain

common characteristics. Although not unchanging, they tend to be somewhat stable operations. They require trained manpower and a good bit of it. These functions are moderately expensive—but worth much more than their cost if well done. They are also severally discrete operations. Although each has an impact on the others, a certain amount of operating autonomy is possible in the conduct of each function. The task of co-ordinating these many specific functions, therefore, is not particularly difficult if it is done in the planning stages, and if it is given reasonable attention. These are the things that Americans have demonstrated that they can do well when they put their minds to it. But they are also activities which it is easy to neglect.

The resurgence of dynamic urban growth of unexpected proportions has created new problems and new demands. The performance of essential services that were once thought to be routine now calls for fresh imagination and creativity. With metropolitan areas running into each other across hundreds of miles of once rural land, the municipal functions present a new challenge—to provide essential services, to preserve amenities from total destruction, to maintain the productive efficiency of "the city," and to do all of this without extravagant use of time and resources. The problem of civil defense is a further complication. With the destructiveness of atomic warfare accepted, with the possibility of hostile attack upon American cities accepted, and with this danger increasingly accepted as a constant element in life today, it is only a matter of time until some provision must be made for civil defense. None of these individual problems presents impossible difficulties. Any one can be solved. But in the aggregate, they present a real challenge, perhaps a critical challenge.

The second category in the problem-solving standard for measuring governing capacity consists of the two great national imperatives, "defense" and "full employment." It is easy to recognize the vastness of the defense problem. It has been a principle preoccupation of American politics since 1941. It has given rise to anxieties which revived and gave new potency to the old fashioned "smear" in American politics. It has absorbed a portion of America's productive energy, which by the standards of any prior period would be judged enormous and preposterous. It takes from two to four years out of the life of our ablest young men. It absorbs from 60 to 70 percent of the budget of the national government in most non-war years. It is a national imperative indeed.

The "full employment" function, which Lippmann once called the "new imperative," is the necessity of making sure that the economy continues at a high level of employment, with reasonable price stability, a rising standard of living, and increasing productivity. A drastically fluctuating business cycle is no longer acceptable to Americans. Politicians, businessmen, labor leaders, farmers, and economists may differ among themselves as to how the new imperative may best be discharged, but there is general agreement that it must be discharged. This point of agreement has been incorporated in the unwritten constitution by the vehement testimony of all parties and all presidential candidates from Willkie to Eisenhower.

The full employment function is unlike the national defense problem in that it is relatively inexpensive. It depends largely on subtle controls and stimuli rather than services. Even the farm subsidies do not amount to very much when measured against the federal budget or the national income; and the "alarming" deficits of the thirties, when direct relief costs were running high, do not add up to a very large part of the postwar national debt. But the full employment and the defense problems are alike in that they require positive anticipatory planning, comprehensive co-ordination of widely ranging governmental and economic activities, immediate recognition of danger, quick and sure response in emergencies, vigorous and sustained follow-up, and above all great wisdom. In these fields, the government must be able to act with moral force (as well as with physical force); it must have the confidence of the nation; and the people must have confidence in each other. This group of functions, therefore, presents greater administrative difficulties and is a greater challenge to governing capacity than the more stable and discrete activities in the first group of municipal functions.

The third category in the problem-solving standard does not consist of separate functions of government. Rather, it is inherent in the functions we have already described, and derives from them and from the nature of man in a democratic society. It might be called the personal imperative. The first of these derived problems is the necessity of conducting all the affairs of government in such a way that the freedom of the individual child, man, and woman is preserved; that he or she has an opportunity to grow and develop; that there is at least an essential minimum of choice in matters of education, employment, social contacts, recreation, personal expression and religion—as well as in politics. Life does not permit unlimited choices; but considerable freedom for the individual is essential to develop men and women with the capacities to sustain this most complexly collective American society. This freedom is both a foundation for American efficiency and one of the valuable end-products of American society. It is both a means and an end, but even if it ceased to be valued as an end, it would have to be kept alive as a means. Responsibility is the great developer of men, and there cannot be full responsibility without freedom.

The second derivative problem is the necessity of maintaining the group-unity of the nation, the communal solidarity, the feeling of oneness among the people at large. In a pluralistic society such as ours, many healthy loyalties exist. But our loyalties to these groups of which we are members must be consistent with our loyalty to our fellow Americans as a whole. They must contribute to the strength and unity of American society rather than compete with it. We must be Americans first, and businessmen, or professional men, or laboring men, or farmers, second. I am sure that there is no need to emphasize this point—it is "elementary"; but it is easy to overlook the fact that divisive loyalties to sub-groups can develop unnoticed. The ultimate threat to American unity is not the sectional-ism of the nineteenth century or the penetration of Soviet fifth columnists in the twentieth. It is rather the possibility of cleavage between vocational groups or economic classes that becomes too sharp and rigid. It is obviously a function of governmental policy and power to see that benefits accrue to all elements in society and that the benefits of no single group are achieved at the cost of serious detriments to all groups and the general public. But, practically, the balancing of benefits and detriments becomes very difficult if class lines are rigid, and class differences become very great.

To maintain the solidarity and the oneness of the political community in a democratic society is just as imperative to the individual as to maintain his own freedom. When this is destroyed the psychological basis for his own security and freedom is also inevitably destroyed.

The fourth major criterion in the concrete measure of capacity to govern is our ability to make an effective contribution, commensurate with America's power and its position, to the well-being of society as a whole, to the wider world in which we live. This essential contribution is probably not possible without a growing understanding of, and sympathy for, other people, and without recognition of the tightening bonds of world-wide interdependence. America will stand or fall with the western world. To put it more accurately, we will continue to thrive as the entire western world grows and develops its resources, its people, its culture. Or we will stagnate and decline if this entire society of which we are a part stops advancing. We cannot isolate ourselves psychologically, economically, or politically.

This is not to say that isolation is dead. It is to say that it never existed in any real sense. The British in 1812 were able to put ashore a landing party—hardly big enough to be called an army—to take over the national capital, and to burn what has consequently become the "White House" with hardly any difficulty at all. Although America never escaped involvement in any major European war, the fictitious character of isolation did not become apparent to many until 1940, when France fell and Britain was fighting desperately for its very existence.

The great depression bears similar testimony to our involvement with all of the western world. Our own economic collapse was reflected throughout the western world. A Germany that was economically depressed while suffering the pangs of defeat became more vulnerable to Naziism than it would have been otherwise. It is possible that the more moderate Bruening regime could have continued in power and kept Germany on a more rational course in dealing with its problems. The impact of economic depression in the aftermath of war swung the balance from moderation to violence.

Why are the words of the President of the United States heard with such joy, or anxiety, throughout the world? Because he has become a leading spokesman of all western society, which consciously or unconsciously recognizes its oneness.

Recapitulating, the concrete measure of capacity to govern consists of four categories of problems: (1) the task of performing numerous specific and now well established municipal functions; (2) the more sweeping and comprehensive national imperatives of "defense" and "full employment"; (3) the derivative problem of performing all of these functions by means that are at the same time conducive to maintaining individual freedom and national unity, the personal imperative; and (4) the problem of making sure that western society of which we are an integral part continues to advance with us, which we may call the international imperative.

These four imperatives, municipal, national, personal, and international, are alike in that each demands to be satisfied; but they present somewhat different problems, and they call for different capacities.

The municipal functions are old or well established, stable, and accepted, although they present a new challenge today. The national imperatives are new, at least in scope and magnitude, unstable, and highly controversial. We had no real defense problems during the nineteenth century, and it was not until the primitive doctrines of violence and ruthlessness were revived, accredited, and adopted as state policy in Nazi Germany and Soviet Russia that there was in any real sense a continuing peril from a dangerous foreign power. Nuclear warfare has, of course, heightened this peril. The imperative of "full employment" is also the by-product of developments in the economy and of corresponding changes in society which are new in the seriousness of their consequences. In dealing with the municipal imperative we have an accepted, although perhaps obsolete, theory used to move ahead with a positive program.

In dealing with both national imperatives we do not take the initiative in a positive program based upon an accepted theory. We are more given to reliance upon emergency countermeasures, and there are many divergent theories as to the nature of the economic and international problems with which we are contending.

The personal imperative has long been recognized in the democratic ideals of equal justice and opportunity, freedom, minority rights, and limited government built into our constitutional system, to which there have been additions steadily over the course of our history. The principle is not new, in its nature; but it presents new problems of application in the rapidly changing conditions of a dynamic world. There are subtleties in this problem which set it apart from the municipal and national imperatives. In this respect the international imperative is like the personal imperative. For the first time in our history we are not only baffled by the behavior of people of foreign cultures which we do not understand, but we also feel somewhat insecure because of our lack of understanding. It is not "our" world; it is "their" world (as well as ours) and we are but a small part of the world community.

The operating problems in dealing with the national and international imperatives differ from those needed to handle the municipal functions satisfactorily. Specifically the difficulties of integration in day-to-day operations are greater. They involve matters of multiple co-ordination, pooling data and knowledge over a wide range, and bringing it to bear upon related matters through informed decisions that lead to consistent and mutually supporting actions which have a cumulative effect. In these areas there seem to be almost no separate programs, and there is decreasing tolerance for "independent" organizations. The machinery of state has to be taken out of over-drive; the grades are too steep, and the surface is too slippery for administrative freewheeling.

General Guides to Probable Capacity

There is no doubt that if America meets these four imperatives successfully (municipal, national, personal, and international) it will have demonstrated its capacity to govern. It will have met the tests of survival and progress. It will have demonstrated that it can make the right decisions, that it can make them in time, and that it can carry them through to a conclusion with general support.

But what are the right decisions? When are they in time? How much wasted effort can be tolerated? What is the nature of support and how much is essential? If we have to go over each policy and each program of government and of society and determine its bearing upon these problem areas, we will reach a judgment that will be very revealing, and have a high degree of validity; but it will be nearly as laborious as governing itself.

What we are looking for is a short cut, some index that will be reliable and valid in measuring probabilities of success, a set of guides to probable capacity. Rushing in where angels fear to tread, I suggest that we can get some idea about America's governing capacity if we consider five phenomena: goals, doctrines, rational structures, authority, and leadership. Don't hope for too much. We still have to make subjective judgments. We are not yet within sight of an automatic scale. But these five phenomena, I believe, give us important clues to capacity.

Goals. A society needs goals to function. It needs goals which challenge, but which also are realistic. Toynbee's thesis is persuasive that it was the existence of a challenge to which primitive men reacted successfully and creatively that brought each civilization into existence. As mastery of nature increases, as we succeed in dealing with poverty, as we gain in controlling disease, as our precautions against fortuitous natural catastrophes become more effective, the challenge of physical necessity recedes, or seems to. Through creative imagination an advancing society must set new goals for itself.

We need goals defined with sufficient precision to be understood by the great majority of people. We need political goals, economic goals, humane goals, and social goals. They need to be challenging. They need to be progressive. That is, one must lead to another. And in a democracy they must be universal. They must be goals which, if achieved, benefit all, at least to an appreciable extent.

Goals create the tensions which are essential to activate man. It is man's capacity to set goals for himself, once he is beyond the range of inescapable compulsion from his physiological drives, that accounts both for modern man and for civilization.

We observe the importance and effect of goals all around us. I suppose that if there is any idea that strikes fear to the heart of an American industrialist, it is the thought that Americans might suddenly cease to want a new car, another dress, or suit, a new refrigerator, a vacation trip to the West Coast, or a new house. It is apparently of some governmental concern, as well, for it is a matter of public policy to permit corporations to charge to the taxpayer (through deductions from income as a necessary business expense) very heavy outlays for very elaborate and outlandish advertising. The theory apparently is that unless Americans are bombarded constantly with commercials from radio, TV, press, periodicals, and billboards they will stop buying. Hence it is a matter of public policy to subsidize Madison Avenue to set consumer goals for Main Street, so that we will not suddenly relax.

There are other even more vivid examples of the power of goals. When faced with the challenge of war, the nation has generated and utilized an enormous amount of energy. It is not exactly a secret that World War II pulled the United States out of the Great Depression, and that in response to that great challenge we got up a momentum that has lasted a long time.

The experience of Russia is also enlightening. Seeking to become an industrial and military power the Russian leaders have in the space of forty years moved from the eighteenth century into a position of leadership in the twentieth. Russia has become a modern industrial state of enormous power. We question their methods on many grounds, but there is little doubt that effectiveness of goals has contributed to their success. We now see the Chinese using the same device: fixing goals, concentrating on them, and keeping them ever in the public mind, in an effort to speed up industrial and technological advancement. We have plenty of questions about the Russian and Chinese use of goals, and there is much that is revolting, but there is little doubt that the goals play an important part in their national life.

How about our own goals? Is goal-setting left too largely to the advertising agencies, and the public relations firms in American society? Are our goals too exclusively matters of consumer goods and services? Have we adequate group, community, national goals? Have we adequate goals in the field of humane affairs —literature, the arts, aesthetic expression generally? Or is this an underdeveloped area in American life, left largely to commercial purveyors of "gracious living"? Are our goals too crudely quantitative and insufficiently qualitative? For example in the great field of education, have we thought too much in terms of more education for more people, and not enough about what kind of education for what purpose?

My own feeling is that while we have done well in setting goals that are universal, and this has been a source of great strength, we have done less well in the progressive adjustment of goals, in setting group goals of a more formal public character, [1] and that our goals

[1] It may be that the failure to deal effectively with urban problems today is influenced in an important way by the absence of adequate goals and of goal-setting machinery. Who has visualized urban life as

perhaps lack balance. We are perhaps still too much in
the mood of the frontier where consumer goods are
scarce, and physical equipment is at a premium. Being
in a position to satisfy such basic needs more generally
and more generously than any other people (and doubtless we shall continue to do so since these satisfactions
create their own new demands), should we not now
take stock, look around us and look ahead, and use
fresh imagination in fixing goals for America?

Doctrines. Whether it be engineering, chemistry,
physics, or politics we have to make assumptions about
the nature of the ingredients we are mixing. As in
physics, empiricism in social science research has run
ahead of theory. We need some unifying and simpli-
fying theory that will help us to sort out what we know
about man, society and government and give us a reasonable grasp of the realities of their relationship. We
need a concept of the political universe that is realistic
and workable, and sufficiently simple to be understood.
Without a guiding doctrine that is at least roughly
approximate to reality, public policy is inevitably
erratic and vacillating. The trial-and-error process of
social learning becomes a random experimentation that
makes slow progress, with resulting confusion and un-
certainty.

There was little progress in public health measures
until the bacteriologists laid the foundation for the germ

---

it ought to be, or could be at its best? Who can visualize or formulate
a goal for the people of any one great metropolitan area? How could
such goals, once conceived, become *public goals?*. We seem to need
both new ideas and new machinery to generate and give effect to them.

theory of disease, a very crude doctrine judged by present knowledge, but the basis for progress in public health that within fifty years had exceeded all prior human history. We will not be able to deal with inflation and depression effectively until increased knowledge of the economy is brought into focus in a more realistic and precise theory than we have so far attained. Essential to all social progress is a more nearly valid and comprehensive doctrine covering man, government, society, and particularly their interrelationships in our own cultural context. We would be content with something even as rough as a Newtonion model; the nuclear edition could wait.

An adequate theory would have to cover a good many points. Let us consider three, by way of example. What are American doctrines as to (1) the nature of government, (2) relations of the individual to the state, and (3) the concept of the public interest? The theories in which we are interested at this stage are not laboratory theories, but ideas on which men act—generally held views, even unvoiced assumptions.

Popular theory leaves much to be desired it seems to me, on the nature of government. If man is a political animal, and government is a natural and essential part of society, then government, in moral character, is "good," not "bad," but honorable, and proper. Logically government should rank well up among the institutions of American society, especially since there have been extended efforts to make government representative, subject to law, and fully accountable to the public.

There is in circulation a quite different theory—that man is Rousseau's noble savage; that government is unnatural, a necessary evil, but evil and not honorable. Even though this is a convenient rationalization for those who are opposed to specific public programs or policies and who would prefer to discredit government than to have it carry out particular programs which they oppose, government as a social process does seem to have a much lower standing in American life than the status to which the importance of its functions would entitle it.

Should only those tasks be committed to government in the United States which government alone can perform? For example, should the national government divest itself of activities which can be performed by nongovernmental agents even if at greater expense? This seems to have been the official doctrine in the mid-1950's. Or should government undertake activities which it can handle more efficiently than can nongovernmental agents? Or should the government go further and undertake any useful social function which it can handle as well as a nongovernmental agent? In its way the idea that government is inherently bad is as damaging to rational decisions as the communist idea that private enterprise is inherently bad. A much more realistic and rational doctrine is needed.

On the relation of the individual to the state, however, it seems to me that we have made clear gains toward a realistic and workable theory, both in law and in the general view. I believe we are moving toward the view that the interests of the individual and the state are reconcilable, that the interest of neither should in principle be subordinated to the other. The necessary sovereign power of the state should be exercised with restraint and pushed no farther than the public interest requires. Similarly the need for restraint and a sense of responsibility is beginning to be recognized in the exercise of individual rights. The relations of individual and society can never be governed satisfactorily by law alone, and neither the state nor the individual should exploit the letter of the law. The ideas of responsible discretion and rational adjustment have been added to the concept of legal rights and sovereign powers in evolving a doctrine of realistic accommodation between man and the state. This seems to me to be an encouraging development.

The concept of the public interest is an increasingly significant concept in American doctrines. It is a necessary concomitant of the growth of official discretion. It suggests that the official vested with discretion has an obligation to use it for the public welfare over and above the letter of the law. Unless there is reality to this concept, both in its obligatory impact and in a rational approach to the facts, it becomes impossible for government to deal effectively with modern problems. Without some such guide, effective in a real sense, it can not escape from the dilemma of arbitrary action on one hand and engulfing red tape on the other.

The public interest has been most talked about in connection with administrative discretion, for administrators most recently have come to exercise delegated powers. But how about judges and legislators? They too exercise delegated powers beyond the limits of any narrow system of mechanical accountability. Beyond the legislators and judges are the political parties, the pressure groups, the labor unions, the business lobbies, and the varied interest groups which have great political power in our system of government, a system which maximizes voluntary action, and voluntary restraint. Can this system continue to function in dealing with present day problems unless the public interest is given increasing weight in all actions of all parties affecting public policy? Personally, I have doubts. But I am encouraged by what seems to me to be the fact that the standard of the public interest comes up more frequently than it once did, is better understood, and is more generally recognized as the ruling standard for guiding discretion. [2]

Rational Structures. After goals and doctrines as guides to probable capacity to govern comes the rational emphasis in the structures, procedures and standards of government. Man is dependent on his reason to approach reality. So is the state. It is hard enough to be rational. It is the function of governmental machinery to make it easier for men collectively to reach rational decisions. Machinery, however, can not me-

[2] Unlike Rousseau's "general will," perhaps, the public interest today is not conceived to be a personified entity, or even a precise abstraction existing somewhere. It is a standard which an individual behaving responsibly in a democratic society must apply, within the sphere where he is free to act, in behalf of the public. It calls for the exercise of intelligence in approaching reality as well as at least a minimum of good will.

chanically compel, it can only encourage, promote, and maximize the probability of rational action. It is highly important that the machinery, procedures, and organic policies of government be so designed as to have this rationalizing influence.

In looking at our machinery of government with this criterion in mind we get an important clue to American capacity to govern. Judicial independence, court rules and procedures, the hierarchy of appeals, and the written opinion all have as their societal function a rigorous logical concentration upon the issues and the facts presented to the court for adjudication under the law. Formalism may defeat reality at times, and archaic practices may need revision, but in general the judicial system is a good example of machinery designed to increase the probability of rational decisions on the merits of issues.

How about the legislative process? Do the composition, organization, and procedure of legislative bodies maximize or minimize rational judgment? Do they contribute to getting at the facts exactly? To what extent has the propaganda or educational role of a legislative hearing impeded its fact-finding function? Do legislative organization and procedures make for rational consideration in the public interest? Is there adequate weighting of the general interest as against particular interests, too much weighting of the general interest, or does legislative machinery overweight the local, the narrow, the particular, and the petty as against the general public interest? If the legislative process does not contribute greatly to a rational approach to reality viewed from the point of view of the public interest, what justification has it as a mechanism for performing any of its functions?

Administrative organization, procedure, and organic policies also must be judged by the same standard of rationality. Does the machinery of government encourage and make it easy for administrators to approach reality in their fact-finding and planning? Does it make rational action easy, natural, and probable, or does the machinery make rational action difficult?

We can apply the rational standard also to the electoral process and to the still more widely diffused processes of opinion-making and consensus-building. What is the level of discussion in electoral campaigns? On what intellectual level do press, radio, and TV approach the public? What is the rational content in words of the commentators and columnists? It is easy to become impatient with reason and yearn for a more visceral approach to politics. But there is no other way in which man can make progress in dealing with the problems of the real world in which he lives. Since logical thought is difficult for all of us, particularly if prolonged, it is necessary that the machinery of government, and the standards of public discussion should stimulate and reinforce man's capacity for rational thought and action. The rational criterion is not the only test of the machinery of government, but it is the most important one.

Authority. The fourth guide to governmental capacity is the phenomenon of authority. This is not a question primarily of force in the sense of coercive power. It is a matter of moral force, decisiveness, and sustained energy. Unless this kind of authority is in evidence the governing capacity of a people is not very high. The police state is *prima facie* evidence of limited governing capacity (in both senses of the term), and it is not a very efficient way of governing. My own belief is that a society can advance only so far in such a system. A point comes at which it must choose between further advancement and its coercive character. The best measure of the progress of Soviet Russia is not Sputnik, the size of its army, steel production, or even the number of Ph.D.'s per annum in nuclear physics. A more significant index to watch if the data were available would be the size of the secret police, and the strength of army garrisons in Soviet cities.

Authority is a subtle thing. If the powers that be have to use physical force very frequently or to deal with very large groups they are lacking in moral force. Yet if they are not prompt and decisive in using force when needed to bring recalcitrants into line, they weaken governmental authority and it becomes necessary to make increasing use of physical force. This is particularly characteristic of a democratic society where there is so much reliance on voluntary compliance with public policy, and voluntary adjustments of individual differences. Those who would comply voluntarily are discouraged from doing so if willful violators of public policy get off scot free.

An interesting question to consider is the authority possessed by particular groups of public officials. What moral force have the courts? Legislators? The Chief Executive? I would suggest the hypothesis that in the past century the authority of the President and also of governors has tended to rise; and that the authority of American legislative bodies including Congress has fallen. You may not agree. But if you do, why do you think these changes have occurred? This is a particularly good question for prospective administrators.

Leadership. The fifth indicator of governing capacity is leadership; and of the five this may be the most significant. If one had to take his eyes off of everything else in American life and could still be aware of the quality, quantity, and trends in leadership, he would have a pretty good idea as to America's capacity to govern.

In view of the importance of leadership as an element of our predictive scale, we are justified in giving it attention, without attempting a comprehensive treatment. As most of you know, the libraries are full of books on this subject—many of them are very good books. A number of these works even tell you how to "do it yourself," and they do it so well that I shall not try to add to their wisdom. Since we already are well supplied with theories of leadership and with manuals for executives, we can limit our consideration to neglected aspects of the leadership phenomenon in our society—points which I think are overlooked.

First of all what do we mean by leadership? Students of administration have made a number of useful definitions which fall into three principal classes. One emphasizes "knowing the business," and stresses wisdom and skill in dealing with very specific situations. In this view leadership is so much a function of the situation that there is not much transferability of leadership capacity. A second more behavioristic view is that leadership is essentially a procedure. "POSDCORB" is an example. It is a procedure which can be learned, and applied in any situation. The third view of leadership is that it is a personal quality, and that it consists largely of the ability to elicit a favorable response from other members of the group. This ability in "inter-personal relations" may be developed, but it is thought to be largely inborn.

If executive leadership is a function of the man, the group, and the situation, as Barnard argues,[3] then it seems to me that there is truth in all three of these views, and that leadership is not a constant but a variable. We should expect to find not one but many kinds of leadership in many differing situations. I rather like a definition of leadership from the point of view of its social function. "Leadership is contributing to the needs of the situation in such a way that the group is more efficient in its internal and external relations, and is more effective in its social functions." This is the kind of leadership that interests us.

In addition to variability, it seems to me, we must recognize that leadership in our society is also widely dispersed. A great many members of our society have leadership functions, at times, or in certain situations. A comparatively large proportion of American adults are both leaders and followers, moving from one role

[3] Chester I. Barnard, "The Nature of Leadership," in Schuyler D. Hoslett, *Human Factors in Management* (Parkville, Mo.: Park College Press, 1946), p. 16.

to another as a normal matter. Some will act in the leader's role much more often than others (this is one aspect of the wide differences in the abilities of human beings), but first hand experience with leadership is comparatively widespread in this country. The prevalence of the voluntary principle in the substructures of American society also means that there is wide experience in the selection and appraisal of leaders. Leaders are in part self-elected, but to an important extent support also is a matter of voluntary action.

In addition to being variable and dispersed, leadership is also multiple when viewed from the perspective of its social function. A half dozen functions may be identified, which can be, but seldom are, in any specific social context, exercised all by one man.

Discovery is the first function. There is the man who says, "Look what I have found," or "This is new," or "This is true."

Interpretation is the next function. The discoverer does not always interpret. Someone else comes along in an educational role, finds meaning in the discovery, and conveys his sense of meaning or importance to others.

Stimulation is the third function. The educator may or may not perform it. Very often this role falls to one who reacts with greater emotional force to new discovery and its newly perceived meaning. He is moved, and he tries to move others. He says "We should do something about this." He may not know what to do but he is sufficiently convinced of the need for action to put on the agitator's mantle.

Invention is the fourth function. The inventor listens to the agitator, notes the interpretation, takes a fresh look at the discovery and comes up with an idea as to what could be done, or with alternatives. He says, "Here are some possibilities."

Catalyzing consensus is a fifth vital function. This function is to facilitate the choice among alternatives and get support for choice. This man has the knack of being able to say, "This would work," or "Why not try this?" and, of getting people to go along on a definite course of action. He facilitates decision.

Organizing co-operative action is a sixth leadership function. The catalyst's contribution may complete the process. But very often it does not. A complex and sustained group effort may be needed to carry through the agreed program. The function of organizing and sustaining co-operative action is very often performed by still another leader. It is vital to effective social action.

This is not a definitive analysis of leadership functions. You could devise a different and longer list of functions that would be equally valid. The point is that there are multiple functions of leadership in both small simple groups, in large complex groups, and in the total complex of society. We have reviewed them as if they were a chain of roles coming one after another in time, like a relay team, and so they are. But some or all of the functions also may be performed more or less simultaneously, and then the team members are performing together, each one preparing for or reinforcing the efforts of the others.

This phenomenon of multiple leadership is widely evident in American society, and particularly in the most dynamic segments of American life. We see it reflected in the proliferation of staff agencies, in committee systems, in the conferences which occupy so much time of administrators. We see it in the steadily increasing delegation and subdelegation of administrative discretion in government, and in the trend toward decentralization in great industrial corporations. We see it also in the way in which decisions are made through the interacting efforts of persons and organizations scattered through legislative bodies, administrative departments, and the public. These men and conditions are reactions to size and complexity and space.

A further point on leadership, which may be easily overlooked, is the rather general and probably increasing desire for meaningful participation in group decisions, even in groups which in the past have not been of democratic structure. [4] Probably this trend should have been expected as the natural product of

[4] Since the Hawthorne experiments of the late 1920's, industrial psychologists and other students of management have been increasingly aware of employee resistance to authoritarian management, i.e., "directive leadership," and the impersonal demands for a depersonalized behavior in industrial organizations. The desire among industrial employees for more personally meaningful participation is now recognized as a significant, although by no means universal phenomenon. See, for example, the interesting article by Rensis Likert, *Developing Patterns of Management,* American Management Association, reprinted for the General Management Series Nos. 178 and 182. See especially I, p. 13 *ff.,* and II, p. 6 *ff.*

A provocative treatment of the individual's response to formal or-the democratic political and social context. The democratic ideal is taken seriously. It does grip men's minds —significant numbers of men—and it has shaped personality development for generations. Here may be an increasing democratic momentum, and a factor of growing significance in American life.

These four aspects of the leadership phenomenon fit together. If leadership had not come to be multiple, dispersed, and varied, the desire to share in the process probably would not have developed to the extent which it has, nor would participation be regarded as a realistic and feasible goal. Cultivation of the latent desire to share in important decisions and actions also makes possible a wider dispersion of leadership functions. Here is a trend which feeds on itself.

In concluding, I would like to ask prospective administrators to do three things:

(1) Applying the pragmatic problem-solving test of capacity sketched in the four imperatives (municipal, national, personal, and international), to determine the areas in which the greatest strength has been shown, and those in which there is the most evidence of weakness.

(2) Using the more abstract predictive index of goals, doctrines, rational structures, authority and leadership (or any other which they prefer), to determine the prob-

---

ganization in industry as a negative defensive reaction is to be found in Chris Argyris, *Personality and Organization* (New York: Harpers, 1957). He sees the personality of the "mature" adult challenged by the impersonal demand for submission and conformity which formal organization imposes. He sees informal organization as a means of defense for the adult personality.

able greatest sources of strength and greatest causes of weakness in governing capacity.

(3) In the light of either or both of these tests, to identify the two or three most serious problems facing America, or to identify the type of problem which is likely to prove most difficult for American capacity to solve.

4. Leadership and the public service

LEADERSHIP IS AN INTRIGUING SUBJECT. It is easy to get lost in pursuing it and to go in circles. We have already noted that in present-day America, leadership is varied, widely dispersed, and multiple in character, and that the desire to share in the leadership process very probably is increasing. If these views approach reality, then the subject is very large indeed and ramifies throughout American life. It would be easy to wander endlessly.

The persuasive argument of Toynbee that leadership is the decisive element in the progress of civilization provides a point of departure for a limited venture into the field. Although Toynbee documents this thesis in 5,000 pages of commentary on the origin, growth, and disintegration of world civilizations, he gives no clue as to the nature of leadership except to say that it is a minority function and that the vital quality is creativity. When the leading minority loses its creativity, it becomes an exploiting minority and the processes of disintegration begin.

Creativity

But what is creativity? In our society today, I suggest that at the higher levels creativity of leaders depends upon five qualities.

1. First is the ability to recognize societal needs, needs of the whole group, needs for action. These needs may be an external "challenge," or an internal challenge, or both.

2. The second quality is an inner compulsion to act in response to the recognized need, and to act in the public interest. Perhaps this is what people mean when they speak of "dedication."

3. The third quality is receptivity to new ideas, approaches, methods. Innovating capacity is desirable in higher societal leadership; but if it is alert and receptive to new ideas, even though they may originate in lower echelons, creativity need not be lost.

4. Fourth is the ability to set goals, goals that are challenging but realistic and which not only meet the specific challenge, but which also inure to the benefit of both the group and its constituent member groups and individuals in so far as this is possible. In all probability the exigencies of life are such that the public whose interests are weighed and benefited must often include even external groups and individuals. Whether we like it or not, we are our brother's keeper. This is now a principle of expediency as well as of moral law; and it may well be inherent in the nature of civilization. The best insurance of civilization in a limited area such as one country is to "shore up" progress at least through-

out the entire civilization; and the best defense against external pressures is to promote individual progress beyond the pale as well.

5. Fifth is the ability to integrate ideas, plans, programs, operations in a rational whole. This is peculiarly necessary in this age when our policies, structures, and institutions have not caught up with the forces of specialization and growth. Fields of knowledge have exploded; industrialization has repeatedly broken through barriers of size and productivity; governmental activities and programs have extended and proliferated; vocational and economic groups find it difficult to communicate, each within itself, and inter-group communications seem to be approaching a new Babel. The development of specialists and experts has kept pace with these trends in nearly all lines. The kind of leadership which is scarce and now has premium value is synthesizing ability, ability to recognize the larger unities, and to fit together the pieces into a rational whole.

My suggestion is that the creativity of societal leadership at the highest levels depends upon these five qualities: (1) ability to recognize needs; (2) inner compulsion to act in the public interest, (3) receptivity to fresh ideas; (4) ability to set challenging and realistic goals in the public interest; and (5) ability to integrate ideas, plans, programs, and operations in a rational whole.

Government's Unifying Role

Turning now to government, we note that its responsibility for exercising a leading and unifying function is becoming (if it has not already become) pre-eminent. It was not always so. Throughout most of the history of this United States of America, government has not been the unifying element in national life. As a people we have, except for a few brief periods of crisis, been economically oriented, not politically oriented. Now the scene has shifted and *public* affairs are increasingly the central focus of national attention. Although the trend in thinking still lags behind the fact of government's crucial role in the nation's life, in more and more of the critical decisions and actions, government is taking the decisive part.

The most important leadership group in America today, I believe, are the governmental leaders. Their decisions and actions are influencing, and in some instances perhaps determining, our future in a most important way. This is not to say that we have, or ever will have, a socialist government (I do not think so). But it is to say that deliberate decisions, definite policies, and specific programs of a national character are needed. They force themselves upon us; and the only responsible agent for national action in the public interest of all is the Government of the United States.

The Importance of Specifications

What kind of leadership does the Government of the United States need? It seems to me that the need is for the sort of creative leadership that we have discussed, and that creativity depends upon the same component qualities. They are needed at the highest levels in all

branches of the government, and in the considerable
group of men who actually are in public affairs because
of their activities and power touching public opinion,
public policy, and public administration, even though
they hold no governmental position.

How can creative leadership of this quality be provided on so broad a front? To answer that question we
shall have to divide it into several parts, and I propose
to take up but one of these, leadership at highest levels
in the executive branch, and primarily one half of this
problem, i.e., leadership of professional administrators.
Before going ahead, however, I think we should note
that it is possible within very broad limits to construct
a system that will produce leaders of any sort we (the
public) want, provided that we define the performance
specifications clearly and take the appropriate measures
to fill them.

It may not be possible to construct a system that will
provide the broadest societal leadership of a creative
character, except the system we have, the policy of trying
to develop individuals for their own sake, and for the
public good, through the opportunities and responsibilities of a democratically oriented free society. This
is the prodigal method of nature. Sow with a generous
hand on a wide front and wait for the harvest!

In organizing a specific body of men for the management of our governmental affairs, however, we have a
definite task, a very limited objective, which there is no
doubt can be accomplished. If any lesson is clear from
history, it is that this kind of social engineering can be
done. It has been done successfully in many different

times in so many different ways that it is clear that the chief requirements are to define the task and set about it energetically. There are some very striking examples in evidence in both ancient and modern history.

The weirdest of these, to men reared in a democratic culture of the twentieth century, are the slave bureaucracies which enabled nomadic invaders to rule great empires in Europe and Africa, and to give their subject peoples peace and order (if not much opportunity for progress). The Janissaries in the Ottoman Empire and the Mamelukes in Egypt were a corps of civil servants, administrators, and soldiers—efficient, highly competent, and well disciplined—who were entirely slaves. [1] They manned even the highest posts in the army and the administration, but they were the slaves of the monarch. They were a potent force whose ability and energy beat down all opposition, domestic and foreign. They were for hundreds of years the most proficient civil and military bureaucracies in the civilized world; but they were slaves. They were recruited from youthful slaves, conscripted, stolen, or captured, most of them of foreign origin; they were converted to a strange religion; and they became the efficient governing machine (civil and military) of an alien conqueror.

The success of this almost incredible personnel system is testimony to man's versatility, cultural dependence, and urge to grow. It was a slave corps, but there

---

[1] *Cf.* Toynbee's treatment of this phenomenon as an adaptation of nomadic herdsmen's use of auxiliaries (horses and dogs) to men (slaves) in tending their flocks (conquered peoples) (*A Study of History*, Vol. III, p. 28 ff.).

was the incentive of advancement to the highest positions of civil and military authority, and the standard
of advancement ruthlessly enforced, was competence.
The Janissary corps eventually degenerated, after it was
watered down by the admission of noblemen's sons, and
the Mamelukes in time became masters as well as slaves,
holding the Caliph as a captive puppet, but they are
monuments to what can be done in creating a personnel
system if the specifications are defined sharply and if
there are sufficiently vigorous measures to fill them.

I am not suggesting that the Janissaries are a model.
They are not. But I am suggesting that if it is possible
for an alien conqueror to devise quickly a personnel
system that will produce highly competent and successful professional administrators of a culturally hostile
empire, it is well within the realm of possibility for a
democratic society to devise a system to provide a fully
competent higher civil service for democratic government. There is no doubt that personnel systems can
be designed to provide almost any type of personnel.
But the first and critical question is to determine what
type is needed. The objective must be clearly established.

Performance Specifications for a Higher Civil Service

Probably the most striking aspect of the history of
American civil service reform is that until quite recently there has been no effort to envisage the sort of a
higher civil service that is needed and desired. The
national personnel system, on which others have been

modeled, more or less, is an evolution, a growth from the bottom up. Beginning in an effort to save the parties as well as the civil service from the corrupting influence of patronage, positions of a standardized type at low levels of responsibility were brought over, one small bloc at a time, into the "classified service," that is a "merit system" which was entered by competitive examination, and in which advancement could be based upon professional competence. The coverage of this "merit system" was extended one step at a time and progressively to positions at higher levels of responsibility, and eventually it began to include positions at high levels, chiefs of bureaus (the major subdivisions of the great departments of government) and administrative assistant secretaries.

In the meantime there were efforts to adapt the machinery of the system to the problems of large-scale employment which accompanied the advent of big government. This adjustment, which has been partially successful, was no mean feat; for the formalities of competitive examinations which were stressed for so long as a necessary ritualistic protection against favoritism, and the centralized personnel controls created for the same purpose, have at times been lacking in both validity and essential flexibility. [2] Not even in this adjustment,

[2] This adjustment of the civil service to mass operations was an important development stemming from Civil Service Commission innovations under pressure of World War II demands, the recommendations of the first Hoover Commission, and the forthright efforts of the Truman administration to implement the personnel recommendations of the Hoover Commission. See the Commission on Organization of the Executive Branch of the Government. *Personnel Management,*

however, was there an effort to visualize the problems of the higher civil service as such and to deal with them. It was assumed almost without thinking that administration at high levels was like administration at low levels, and that the status, procedures, and policies governing the employment of clerical office workers were equally appropriate for directors of vast regional organizations, heads of important divisions, and chiefs of great bureaus. The higher civil service was in a blind spot of the public eye (of reformers, experts, politicians, administrators, all alike). It was neglected.

This neglect is in sharp contrast to the rest of the world's experience. Where the challenge of new governmental problems, or the pressure of expanding functions upon limited resources has stimulated civil service reform, the simplest and quickest way to get results, and the way that has been followed almost universally has been to create a higher civil service of a sort deemed to be desirable, and largely to entrust further reforms of the rest of the civil service to this reformed group. The higher civil service has been used to tone up the efficiency of the civil service more generally.

This is also the historic policy of the United States in developing professionally efficient military forces. Academies to train officers were established at West Point, Annapolis, and Colorado Springs. An officer corps was established for Army, Navy, and Air Force, and great attention was given to the selection and ad-

---

February 1949, and *Task Force Report on Federal Personnel,* January 1949.

vancement of officers into the higher ranks. Once these steps were taken, it was relatively simple to entrust the creation and administration of competent armed forces to the higher military servants drawn from the officers' corps. I am not suggesting that the military is a model for the civilian. But it is clear that in creating an efficient body of public servants on a large scale, the almost universal practice has been to give the most thought to the highest positions, and to take the greatest pains to make sure of the high qualities of the men in them. The exception is the United States civil service. The present methods of dealing with higher civil servants are not a system designed for that purpose; they are an inadvertence.

In thinking about the specifications for a higher civil service it is wise to note that functions of leadership in any effective system of administration in a democratic society are divided between the political executives who come and go and the professional administrators who make government a career. This is an instance of the combination of voluntarism and professionalism that runs through our society. Or, if you prefer, it is an example of combining two different kinds of professionalism. Either way it is a general problem.

We have noted that voluntarism is a pronounced phenomenon in a democratic society, and in this respect the United States may lead the world. We have noted also that the forces of specialization and professionalization run strongly in an advanced society. Here too America cannot be far behind the head of the procession. We are known for the number and vitality of our voluntary associations, special-purpose organizations created for very special purposes. They are quickly conceived, rapidly set on their feet, and almost at once they are off and running. But how is this done? If the goals are ambitious and if the enterprise is substantial, a very early step is to bring in a professional secretary or director who creates a professional secretariat which largely operates the voluntary association! Look about you at the famous voluntary organizations—the Red Cross, the Y.M.C.A., the Chamber of Commerce, the labor unions, and the American Society for Public Administration, for examples. A professional staff increasingly gives leadership to the associations, volunteers relax into a nominal role, and make only perfunctory contributions to leadership. Perhaps this frees them for new voluntary efforts. They keep their freedom of action and room for maneuver. Does this trend, if it is a trend, make the voluntary associations more or less effective? [3] Does the increasing proportion of professionalism in their leadership make them less voluntary, or merely more efficient?

These questions suggest to us the general nature of the problem of combining professional and nonprofessional staff in public affairs organizations. Nowhere is the question more important than in government,

[3] It may be noted that the professionalization of business management is generally thought to have gone much farther. The "voluntary" owners of most great corporations now exercise little control of them. There are only a few in which individual or family control still continues, and its sole effective function seems to be the selection of the professional manager-in-chief.

where it is a vital part of the democratic character of government. Placing the highest executive authority and responsibility in the hands of men who are dominantly "public" men, who are not experts in the technology which they supervise, and who are expected to come and go from the administration, is an established part of our constitutional system. It is an institutionalized practice that must continue until replaced by something better for the same ends—and there is nothing in sight. At the same time the demands of professionalization have thrust themselves upon us. It is not possible to operate an establishment such as the executive branch of the government of the United States without experienced, expert, trained, skillful professional administrators at all key spots, even, and particularly, at high levels. The professionals cannot take over command, but neither can the political executive in charge operate without them. It is clear that the talents of the political executive and the professional administrator must be blended. The question is, how and at what levels can they best be combined?

Both political executives and professional administrators need the creative qualities that we have considered (recognition of needs, compulsion to act, and ability to motivate others, receptivity to new ideas, ability to set goals in the public interest, and integrating ability). The functions of creative leadership must be shared, and this seems to me to be the important starting point. The contribution and emphasis may well be different. For example, in setting goals, the political executive may be more conscious of the need for new policies, while the professional administrator may be more aware of the need for perfecting or extending established programs. In defining the public interest, the political executive may be very conscious of "raw desire," immediate pressures, and contemporary considerations, while the professional administrator may weigh more heavily past precedents, long run consequences, and considerations of cost and feasibility. Despite such differences in emphasis both the political executive and the professional administrator must be creative in their leadership.

The functions of the professional administrator in his supporting but subordinate role (his greater technical competence, his longer experience, his more intimate knowledge, and his continuing status) create special needs in addition to the basic need for creative leadership. Some of these, it seems to me, are:

1. Counseling skill—ability to give wise counsel to their political superiors on all matters of both policy and operations on which the civil servants have experience and insight. This would include matters of dealing with committees of Congress, interest groups, and the public. Experience is a good teacher in these subjects and the career administrators have been "in" on a good many lessons. This skill ideally should include at least a trace of real diplomacy, the art of making unwelcome news or views palatable.

2. Operating skill—ability to get things moving and keep them running. The compulsion to act in the face of need, for these men, should include the ability to communicate the sense of urgency to others. Political

executives ought not to have to get into normal operations. New policy and changes of pace or directions—
yes. But day-to-day administration—no.

3. Integrating ability. Although we have defined
this as an element of all creative leadership, and it is
needed in political executives as well as professional
administrators, it is almost impossible to be sure that it
will be found in sufficient strength among the come-
and-go political executives. Public policy should
compensate by making doubly certain that higher civil
servants are devoted to the national interest and not
particular interests, to the government and not particular departments, and to the department rather than to a
component bureau. The forces of particularism are so
strong, expressed through organized outside pressures,
and through the institutional momentum of specialized
interests within bureaus and divisions, that unless the
higher civil service exercises a strong unifying influence
the public interest may be subordinated to the interest
of well organized and energetic special interests. Organizational arrangements are not enough to keep these
centrifugal forces under control. Personal integrating
leadership of the higher civil service, trained to recognize and defend the broader interests, is essential to
achieve such an integration in fact, and especially to
compensate for the considerable barriers to unified
planning and integrated operations which the looseness
of the machinery of government creates.

Unifying leadership of this sort depends to a considerable extent on a combination of fundamental integrity
and intellectual breadth or vision. An administrator

must be able to see the broader public considerations even in issues which are narrowly presented, and he must be faithful to the more general interest even though the proposals of special interests are most vehemently urged.

4. Integrity of a subtle character is in fact an essential virtue of leadership in the higher civil service, a quality that can be sensed although not always appreciated by superiors, subordinates, and colleagues: veracity; candor tempered by good will; subordination of self (when necessary) to the good of the organization and the cause; courage to take necessary risks, both personal and official, tempered with prudence to avoid danger.

5. Going still further into the subtle and subjective world I would say that higher civil servants need the quality of faith—that truth can be and will be (at least ultimately) recognized; that the reasonable approach and the rational view will prevail; that men around them will identify with the common cause which it is their mission to administer; that there is sufficient good will among them to make the necessary adjustments, to make allowances for honest mistakes, to contribute the extra energy when needed, and even to sacrifice when much is at stake. This kind of faith (or philosophy, if you prefer) is contagious. It can infuse an entire organization and lift its effectiveness to a higher level, measured both in product and internal satisfactions.

These are the specifications, as I see them, for a higher civil service in the national government. I should like to turn now to the proposals to deal with the question of a higher civil service in a systematic way, the proposals of the second Hoover Commission and its Task Force on Personnel and Civil Service which reported to the Congress in January 1955. In discussing these proposals, I shall draw upon the more detailed Task Force report which the Commission very largely adopted and endorsed.

The Higher Civil Service Today

The Task Force on Personnel and Civil Service noted that:

1. Higher civil servants of demonstrated competence and integrity are not identified individually or as a group.

2. Regardless of long and successful performance they have only job security, not career status.

3. Higher civil servants do not have a generally recognized standing in American society appropriate to their responsibilities, and they are at times subject to widespread charges of incompetence and partisanship. These charges are more frequent and extreme when a President of one party succeeds the administration of a President of another party, but they are not limited to such times.

4. The civil service system, originally intended for the control of gross patronage in lower ranks, and adapted to problems of mass employment in relatively standardized positions, is not well designed for civil servants at high levels of administrative responsibility where the qualities of the man more largely determine

the job. It gives less flexibility in assignment of higher civil servants than is desirable, and also less certain status in a governmental career.

(In the Task Force view a personnel system, particularly for dealing with men at high levels of responsibility, is only a part of the broader management process. Management questions and personnel questions must be dealt with together.)

5. There are heavy demands upon top management in the national government where the complexities of congressional politics and the avid interest in details of administration of the many committees and subcommittees, not to mention the myriad organized pressures, generate great centrifugal force and make for a large volume of work.

6. The President has a pivotal role as responsible chief executive in maintaining the strength and unity of the government; the trend of public policy in recent years is to strengthen departmental management under the Chief Executive as an essential link in the chain of responsibility and authority.

7. The Task Force found that a combination of circumstances had made for a confusion of functions within top management in which frequently there tended to be an inadequate distinction between the obligations and activities of responsible political executives and those of administrators who were presumed to be or who wished to be permanent civil servants. This confusion resulted in publicly involving these professional administrators in politics to such an extent that color was given to the charge that the higher civil service gen-

erally was partisan in its official behavior, the careers of individual civil servants were jeopardized, and political executives lacked the stable administrative support which they required from experienced higher civil servants. In some instances the participation of civil servants with competitive status in political functions, doubtless, was voluntary and deliberate, but more often it was the result of failure of political leadership to meet its responsibilities and the shifting of its proper functions by default to subordinates. The net result of this situation was to weaken top management in the government, to blur responsibility, and to place both political leadership and higher civil servants in a disadvantageous position.

Major Proposals of the Hoover Commission

To deal with problems of the higher civil service in the broad context of top management, the Task Force on Personnel and Civil Service first proposed a clearer division of functions between political executives and career administrators, in which political executives would carry the burden of active advocacy and defense of the decisions and actions of the administration, a burden which goes with political responsibility. In line with the recommendations of the first Hoover Commission, the reforms of both the Truman and Eisenhower administrations, and the opinion of many students of administration, it strongly recommended that the responsibilities and functions of political leadership be concentrated at the departmental level, and that man-

agement at the subordinate bureau level take a supporting role. It saw very clearly that if both departmental
executives and bureau administrators are politically
active, real authority reverts to the bureaus, departmental direction and control are enfeebled, and with
them the Chief Executive's strength, which is essential
to our system of government. It also saw that if the
distinction between the political executive and the
professional administrator is not made between the department and the bureaus *in the line of command,*
bureau management tends to lack the experience and
skill which are required to deal with its subtle combination of pressures and technics, and that the ceiling
for the career service inevitably is depressed below the
bureau level. With such a low ceiling for advancement,
it would be impossible to attract and hold in the Government of the United States civil servants of the high
capacities which now are needed.

It should be noted that the Task Force did not say
that policy and administration can be separated. On
the contrary it noted that administrators are necessarily
vested with discretion at many levels, and there are
many levels of policy. Nor did the Task Force attempt
to exclude professional civil servants from the departmental management. It made specific provision for
them in auxiliary staff positions up to and including
the administrative assistant secretary and the deputy
chief of staffs concerned with substantive policies. It
was the view of the Task Force that departmental management needs both political executives and professional
administrators to be fully effective; but the former

should have the responsibility for and the function of command.

The second recommendation, of the four major proposals, was to strengthen top management by taking steps to increase the supply of qualified political executives. The problems are more difficult, the burdens are heavier, and the necessary skills are greater than generally has been realized. The political executive's job is one of the most difficult and important in our society. Yet we lack a system to find and develop talent. There are plenty of executives and plenty of politicians. But how to get the two strains crossed is the question. The Task Force did not pretend to know the answer to this problem; but it did suggest some first steps and urge action.

It is not until we reach the third recommendation that we come to the Task Force proposal for a senior civil service—"a group of professional administrators carefully selected from all parts of the civil service and from all departments and agencies solely on the basis of demonstrated competence." [4]   It recommended that they "have status, rank, and salary as individuals" and be "employed flexibly in a number of authorized positions calling for high administrative talents." "The primary objective," it said, "is to have always at hand in the Government a designated group of highly qualified administrators whose competence, integrity, and faithfulness cannot reasonably be questioned; who will make it easier for political executives to discharge their

---

[4] *Task Force Report on Personnel and Civil Service,* pp. 50-51.

responsibilities, and who will add to the smoothness, the effectiveness, and the economy of governmental operations. A secondary but related purpose is to make the civil service more attractive as a career to able men and women." To this latter end the Task Force also recommended substantial increases in pay and retirement benefits.

The senior civil service proposal was developed in some detail so that the idea would be understood and not brushed aside. But the Task Force stated explicitly that it did "not emphasize details of the proposal" and that it was aware that "the plan may be improved in operation." However, it was "strongly convinced that action of the general nature outlined should be taken promptly and carried through until it is firmly established in the institutional framework of the Government." [5]

This brings us to the last but not the least of the four major recommendations—on training and executive development. The Task Force said rather emphatically, "What is needed is a straightforward and vigorous effort to develop the capabilities of civil servants generally in their technical, vocational, professional, and managerial knowledge and skills. But particular emphasis is needed on building up the executive capacities of the civil service in a systematic executive development program which will directly improve the quality of first-line supervision and junior executives, and which also will increase the supply of experienced and

[5] *Ibid.*, p. 51.

competent career administrators for top management posts." [6]   This program also was outlined in some detail so that it would not be passed over as vague or incomplete. It was regarded as essential to the success of the four-part program.

Criticisms of the Senior Civil Service

Criticisms of the senior civil service may be summarized under four headings: (1) It is intrinsically a bad idea. (2) It might be dangerous. (3) It is not necessary. (4) It cannot be done.

The senior civil service is intrinsically a bad idea, say some, because it would require too much neutrality of career administrators. This argument is advanced chiefly by academicians who served a happily exciting tour of duty in the federal government once upon a time. It should be noted at this point that the Task Force did not say that politics and administration can be separated or should be in top management decisions. It did say that political responsibilities and corresponding activities of superiors can be separated from administrative responsibilities of a subordinate in top management. The professional administrator, subordinate to a political executive, may be more sophisticated politically than his superior, and he can share this wisdom; but he should not take over the political executive's responsibilities or duties.

---

[6] *Ibid.,* pp. 78-79.   Chapter IV, "Training and Executive Development," is entirely devoted to this theme, and outlines the essentials of an adequate program.

Some critics have argued that a senior civil servant would have to be without feeling or emotion. This was not the position of the Task Force. It spelled out in detail public *activities* to be avoided by senior civil servants; but on the subject of feelings it said simply that "Senior civil servants as a group should be fully prepared to serve faithfully each administration that takes office. This means that they must avoid such emotional attachment to the policies of any administration that they cannot accept change." Could anyone ask a career administrator for less neutrality?

One or two critics go much further and seem to argue there should be no distinction between the activities of political executives and career administrators at any level—that all civil servants at all levels are obliged to support their programs by all means. If accepted, these views would either prevent change of policy by democratic processes, or they would destroy a career civil service entirely. One would have to choose between democratic change and an expert service.

The charge that the senior civil service would be a closed corps, and therefore bad, has been made. On the contrary, it would be open "to all parts of the civil service . . . all departments and agencies." The only restriction is "demonstrated competence" and the low requirement of five years of service. It is not "closed" if civil servants can get into it on their merits after normal advancement to positions of important responsibility.

In a similar vein some have called the senior civil service undemocratic, an "elite," hence bad. Is it undemocratic to recognize merit and achievement demonstrated in the public service? Is it undemocratic to reward outstanding achievement with an adequate salary and reasonable security? If so, American democracy has been operating on a mistaken understanding of the term for a very long time.

There is the peculiar argument that the senior civil service is a bad idea because it would leave out some people. It would not include specialists; it would not include the lower ranks; and hence the people left out would be unhappy. The amount of unhappiness perhaps would be minimized by the fact that specialists would not expect to enter a category not designed for them. Without expectation there need be no disappointment. People with administrative responsibilities in lower ranks could qualify in due course as they advance and therefore need not be unhappy about the existence of a service which they have not yet entered.

But it may be argued, some will not qualify who hope to. This is undoubtedly correct. But is it significant? There are plenty of classifications and categories in the civil service now, and not everyone gets as high as he would like to. But this has not yet been advanced as a reason for repealing the classification act or abolishing the Civil Service Commission.

The second type of criticism of the senior civil service is that although the idea is not inherently bad, powers might be abused, and therefore the senior civil service is too dangerous to attempt. Some fear that a President, never the incumbent, might at some future time in some way abuse his powers with reference to the senior civil service.　This is difficult to follow since the President would have no more power over higher civil servants than he has today.　Others profess to fear that the senior civil service will in some fashion control admission to its own ranks, and will in some improper way become exclusive.　This argument also is difficult to follow; for the proposed administrative arrangements provide for departmental nominations which brings the political executive into the process (a potentially useful lay element), a board in charge with a majority of the members from outside the government, and designation by the President.　These arrangements would tend to restrain such bureaucratic tendencies as may exist within the higher civil service.

Some have argued that the senior civil service would endanger its own membership by calling attention to their existence.　I believe that this argument fails to take into account the nature of political storms in the American scene.　When civil servants draw down the lightning it is because of the high positions they occupy, the functions they perform, and sometimes their personal behavior.　The thunderbolts, moreover, are thrown by interested parties who dislike decisions or actions which have been taken, even though the bolts emerge from clouds of talk about party loyalty.　Actually the Hoover Commission recommendations should deflect many of these blows by shifting the function of political decision and political debate more clearly to the shoulders of political executives.　It is reasonable to expect that the distinction of the men first appointed to the senior civil service will bring credit not discredit

upon it, and that this high standing will be safeguarded
by due care in subsequent appointments as the service
grows to its natural limits. Association with other men
of demonstrated capacity and integrity never distracts
from one's own standing.

Last of all, there is the (to me incredible) argument
that the senior civil service "might—probably would"
—work in reverse: that it would weaken the President's
leadership; increase the power of particular interests
and generally strengthen particularistic forces in the
government. This does not seem to me to be a rational
conclusion. It runs counter to the probabilities as I
understand them, and ignores the facts as I have observed them. Unless the design outlined carefully by
the Hoover Commission were completely disregarded,
and unless the President who implements the program
were inconceivably inept, the senior civil service would
strengthen the Chief Executive's ability to give unity to
his administration and to make it responsive to his
leadership. The senior civil service would tend to exert
this unifying influence because of its (eventual) broader
training, more varied experience, government-career
status instead of bureau-job status, and greater over-all
security growing out of the officially recognized role,
easy transferability and wider range of useful assign-
ments. Moreover, the Chief Executive would name the
board that creates and maintains the senior civil service,
and within the limits of the design he could emphasize
the broadly unifying function of the senior civil service.
The argument of reverse effect has been seriously advanced, but I cannot take it seriously.

The third general criticism of the senior civil service is that it isn't necessary. All is well on the Potomac. The standing of civil servants generally is high enough. The business community's mistrust of civil servants has been replaced by full confidence. The next transition from the administration of one party to that of another will be smooth and easy; and higher civil servants will have no problems. This is an opinion to which those who hold it are fully entitled. But it is based upon faith which I do not share and presumes a number of facts for which at the present time I see no real evidence.

The declarations of high esteem for public servants which many eminent businessmen made when leaving the government after World War II had no effect upon the businessmen who came in to take up the reins of government seven years later. Nor will the endorsements of the Randalls and the Worthys be remembered in the next transition. Schedule C has pushed political appointments well down into bureau management in many departments; and the belief that exists (whether or not it is true) that the present administration has sought to put Republicans in high places even within the classified service will not make the next transition easier. The difficulties of transition will be no less the next time, and they may even be greater than in '53, if steps are not taken in the meantime of a constructive character. [7]

[7] The argument that there is no need for a senior civil service began with two members of the Hoover Commission itself. Representative Clarence J. Brown, in his dissent took the position that the "super

A fourth general criticism of the senior civil service accepts or passes over the merits of the proposal and simply argues "It can't be done." It is said that Congress will not permit the senior civil service to be set up. It is said that higher civil servants will not give up political functions. It is said that political executives at the departmental level will not pick up the burdens of political leadership.

In considering the assertion that it can't be done we should remember that this argument is always advanced when something new is proposed. If the statement were revised to say "It can't be done easily," or "It can't be done without leadership," or "It can't be done without a fight," I would be inclined to agree. But with leadership and intelligent hard work, I believe that the senior civil service can be established—if it has the merit of meeting a real need. In my opinion the argument reverts to the merits of the proposal.

Counterproposals

Three alternatives to establishing the senior civil service have been proposed. One is to stand pat and do nothing. The second is the so-called program-staffing idea. The third is the Career Executive Program developed by the Eisenhower administration.

---

grades" are all that is needed. (This argument was echoed later by incumbents of GS-18 and 17 positions. "What do we have to gain?") Representative Chet Holifield also dissented, seeing "no compelling reason" for a senior civil service. Possible dangers and difficulties also loomed large in the view of these dissenters.

A do-nothing policy implies either perfection in the present system or lack of interest in progress. Since no one seriously argues that the present system as it affects higher civil servants is yet near perfection, the proposal seems to me to lack appeal; and I do not see why it should be accepted by thoughtful men.

"Program Staffing"

The program-staffing idea is, I believe, a by-product of successful emergency measures during the New Deal and World War II when many men and women went into the government temporarily, carried important responsibilities, and after the crisis returned to private life. The proposal as I understand it is to bring in regularly from outside the government executives to man the key positions immediately under the department heads. These would include a considerable stratum at the bureau level and below. By definition they would not be career civil servants, but would be outsiders chosen for their supposed ability to contribute to their respective "programs."

Several observations may be made. The first is that this would put a low ceiling on a civil service career, and as such it would be a severe, perhaps mortal, blow to a career service. Second, it would require a very large number of outsiders to keep these posts filled. The turnover is high in such appointments, and it is particularly hard to keep the most capable men. There is no evidence that it would be possible to secure people who would be an asset to the government in these large

numbers.   Political executive talent of this sort is in
very short supply.   Third, by definition their loyalties
would be to their programs (and their patrons)—not to
the administration or the government as a whole.
Would they not tend to aggravate the problem of
excessive centrifugal forces in our national administration?   They would certainly not increase the unity of
the government.   A fourth probability is that they
would not be very effective.   Those of us who served
in the national government in one of the past emergencies take some satisfaction in having done so and
fondly remember our successful moments.   It is easy to
forget the break-in period and the mistakes we made.
Or we compare our performance with that of the civil
service of the '30's, not with the improved civil service
of the '50's.   What was necessary for past emergencies
is not good enough to meet the normal loads and problems of the present and the future.

The semantic confusion here, also, should be noted.
The advocates of program staffing in their hoped for
"buffer zone" say that because the appointees might
not have had an active party affiliation, these executives would not be "political."   In the thinking and
terminology of the Hoover Commission, however, they
would be political executives if their *function* is politi
cal.   Function, rather than past personal affiliation, is
controlling in their use of the term "political executive."

The idea of "semipolitical executives" occupying a
"buffer zone" accepted by career administrators, party
officials, and members of Congress seems slightly ridicu
lous to others than its devotees.   As David and Pollock

have pointed out, the prospects of building a personnel system on this idea are not very good. [8]

Finally, it is in order to recall that the Hoover Commission did not oppose lateral entry into the classified civil service, or recommend its curtailment. Some lateral entry is always useful and at times essential; but if it is more than a supplementary device, there is something wrong with the personnel system.

Career Executive Program

The Career Executive Program was the Eisenhower administration's first step toward a senior civil service. The presumption was that eventually it would go farther in that direction; but it was not committed to doing so unless experience justified the move.

The Hoover Commission proposed the senior civil service in January 1955. One year later, after mature reflection upon the recommendation within the administration, the President by letter directed his principal personnel adviser to propose a program to implement the senior civil service recommendation which in his judgment, it is reported, is "one of the most far-reaching and imaginative proposals made by the Commission." [9] Then began the long process of consultation for which the administration has become famous. Its low pressure efforts to secure unanimous support within the

[8] Paul T. David and Ross Pollock, *Executives for Government* (Washington: The Brookings Institution, 1957), p. 157.

[9] Philip Young, "A Forward Look in Personnel Administration," Address at the 1956 Annual Conference of the Society for Personnel Administration (U. S. Civil Service Commission, pamphlet), p. 5.

executive branch put a premium on recalcitrance, so that the genius of the experts was directed not to devising ways of overcoming difficulties or weaknesses, but to surveying obstacles and imagining hazards. Mole hills became mountains which had to be climbed one by one, not without some foot dragging on the expedition. The rivers of perspiration that flowed from this effort seem to have washed away some of the White House enthusiasm for the project. But it persevered.

A pilot program formulated by the Civil Service Commission was torpedoed by the departmental experts in February 1956 and sank without a trace. In May of 1956 the President's principal personnel adviser reported that an executive order was in preparation to implement phases of the proposal which did not require legislation. Seven months later agreement was reached, not to take action, but to constitute a committee to recommend what action to take. Again moving without precipitate haste, an executive order was formulated and presented to the White House in April of 1957. In due course, that is, four months later, the order was signed creating what afterwards came to be called the Career Executive Committee. The committee presented its proposals and draft executive order to the White House in late December or early January 1958, and on March 4 the order was signed to establish the Career Executive Board, which in turn was to carry out the Career Executive Program.

Only then did it become apparent that in more than three years of consultation no one had got around offi-

ially to telling the House and Senate Committees on
Post Office and Civil Service what the administration
was up to. A full opportunity to do so, however, was
shortly provided in hearings arranged by the House
subcommittee on Manpower Utilization. The general
effect of the questions then asked was to create the im-
pression that members of the committee felt that this
oversight was most unkind.

Executive Order 10758, of March 4, 1958, created a
career executive service and a Career Executive Board
to launch it. In the words of the order

'Career executive service' means those line or staff positions in the competitive civil service having significant
administrative or managerial characteristics which are
designated by the heads of the executive agencies concerned
with the approval of the Career Executive Board hereinafter established from among (1) positions in grades GS-16
and above (and their equivalents) and (2) positions in
such grades below GS-16 (and their equivalents) as are
hereafter designated, under the authority of this subsection,
as additional career executive-program grades by the United
States Civil Service Commission (hereinafter referred to as
the Commission) upon the recommendation of the said
Board. [10]

At the outset, according to the order, the career executive service would cover super-grade positions within the

[10] "Executive Order No. 10758 of March 4, 1959, Establishing a Career Executive Program Within the Civil Service System," Sec. 1 (a),
*Manpower Utilization in the Federal Government (Career Executive
Program)*, Hearings Before the Subcommittee on Manpower Utilization of the House Committee on Post Office and Civil Service, 85 Cong.
sess. (1958), p. 6.

classified service which are administrative in character
Persons to be designated by the President as career
executives would be recommended by the departments
and agencies and screened by the Board. The Board
also would maintain a roster of such talent with appro
priate "service and experience records"; it would de
velop methods for the regular appraisal of performance
it would assist the agencies in devising training pro
grams to increase the supply of executive talent; and i
would recommend to the Civil Service Commission
"changes in position classification practices to permi
greater flexibility in the assignment of career execu
tives." It may be noted that the Board was designed to
operate in co-operation with the Civil Service Commis
sion, and to depend heavily on assistance from the
Commission's staff. The Board's recommendations for
changes in civil service rules and for legislation would
go to the President through the Commission.

The Board as first constituted consisted of five mem
bers, three from private life and two from within the
government. Members Arthur S. Flemming, Charles B
Stauffacher, and James H. Taylor were from private life
and Frederick J. Lawton and James P. Mitchell were
from the government. When Mr. Flemming became
Secretary Flemming, the 3-2 nongovernmental majority
was reversed. On August 6 the board was enlarged by
the addition of two nongovernmental memberships to
restore the lay predominance. One of these was filled
eventually by the appointment of James E. Webb.

The administration took the position that the Career
Executive Program was a first step toward the senio

civil service proposed by the Hoover Commission. There would be no rank-in-person, no enhanced procedural protection for security, no added obligations, and no superior pay or fringe benefits. It was argued that the appointment procedure and presidential designation would bring increased prestige and security, that the proposed revision of classification practices would make for greater flexibility in assignment, and that the Board's roster of talent would increase opportunity for and availability of career executives. These seemed to be reasonable expectations for this modest first step. The administration proposed to go on from there in the light of experience, a conservative procedure.

How far would it go? This was not an easy question to answer in 1958. Members of the House Subcommittee on Manpower Utilization in interrogating administration witnesses on the career program took two quite different positions. One was that it was dangerous, would create a privileged "elite," might be exploited by a future President, and could become a vehicle for bureaucratic independence. It also looked hard for evidence that the discretion of department heads might be impaired (a new worry for congressmen). The second position was that the Career Executive Board would not do anything that the Civil Service Commission itself could not do without an executive order, and that the Board and the program are unnecessary. The chairman of the subcommittee, after the hearings, but in advance of the subcommittee's report, issued a press release (July 27, 1958) announcing a subcommittee resolution "that no activity to further the

creation or administration of the career executive program be taken until the subcommittee has had a chance
for further study in the 86th Congress." Copies were
sent to the Civil Service Commission and the White
House.

At this point the Administration was faced with a
choice. It could yield ignominiously to the stop order
of a House subcommittee chairman, abandoning the
program developed so carefully over a period of nearly
four years. It could seek to win over the committee
opposition, pushing ahead steadily within the area of
the President's authority as planned. Or it could act
boldly, make a strong case for the idea, and seek posi
tive legislative support for a more ambitious program.

The last course of action apparently was not con
sidered. What actually happened was a disappointmen
from many points of view. The Administration in
tended to win over the committee chairman through
face-to-face discussion of the merits of the Career Execu
tive Program, but successive efforts to do so miscarried
In the meantime a small but quite competent staff fo
the Board was borrowed from the Department o
Health, Education, and Welfare and from the Civi
Service Commission; an "administrative committee" o
career administrators was formed to advise the Board
and regulations to activate the program were prepared
and approved by the Board. But the further steps to
set the program in motion were deferred until the con
flict with the House subcommittee could be settled
The subcommittee chairman, however, did not tem
porize; he went ahead with steps to strengthen the sto

order through action of the House Committee on Appropriations. In reporting the appropriation both for the Department of Labor and the Department of Health, Education, and Welfare, the Committee report stated, "The Committee directs that none of the funds contained in the bill be used for the support of this [Career Executive] Board's activities." [11] This was an action, which, although extralegal, was more immune to legislative revision than an actual rider to the bill, since it could not be dealt with on the floor or in the Senate. In the Independent Offices Appropriation Bill, reported May 8, 1959, a rider was attached to the appropriation for the Civil Service Commission which "Provided, That no part of this appropriation shall be available for the Career Executive Board. . . ." [12]

When confronted with this direct challenge, the Administration chose not to fight for the Career Executive Board. The staff was released June 30, 1959, and the only question remaining was whether to revoke Executive Order 10758 or to allow the Board to wither on the vine.

In retrospect this denouement seemed to some observers to be the pathetic but not entirely unexpected consequence of the highly recommended policy of "incrementalism," [13] applied by an administration which

[11] *Department of Labor . . . Appropriation Bill, 1960,* House Committee on Appropriations, Rept. 309, 86 Cong. 1 sess. (Apr. 28, 1959), p. 2.
[12] *Independent Offices Appropriation Bill, 1960,* House Committee on Appropriations, Rept. 350, 86 Cong. 1 sess. (May 8, 1959), p. 13.
[13] David and Pollock, pp. 109-11.

had not come to be known for vigorous leadership. A most carefully developed and modest program said to have full presidential support was stopped dead by the chairman of a subcommittee of a House committee standing close to the bottom of the prestige scale. What a dismal defeat for a General of the Armies, twice elected to the Presidency with historic victories over one of the strongest candidates ever to be defeated. Did not the President and his Career Executive Program deserve a better fate?

Some intangible achievements may be noted. In the course of the four and a half years most of the career administrators who had opposed the idea of a senior civil service at the outset came to understand it, and to see its merits. But unfortunately their success in opposing the idea in 1956 and 1957, when the Administration probably could have moved effectively, was much greater than their success in supporting the Career Executive Program in 1958 and 1959 when the favorable moment for action had passed, and when the Administration was running out of gas. Still more unfortunately there was not much observable progress in explaining the program to Congress, either to the membership in general, or to the hostile subcommittee in particular.

The Problem Remains

The problem of the higher civil service remains, and is approaching an acute condition. The civil service as a whole has made great advances over the past generation. But these have not been the consequence of organizational or institutional arrangements designed for, or of particular benefit to, the higher civil servant. The latter is still employed just as is a clerk, messenger, or building guard. Despite the responsibilities he carries, the burdens he bears, and the leadership expected of him, he has no better status and no more of a "career" than the least responsible office worker. He is never more than the employee of a bureau, division, or office, and never as much as a servant of Uncle Sam. The young man entering the federal service has nothing to look forward to except a succession of specific jobs, in which he will have to move against the stream, not with it, if he is ever to have experience outside of a single bureau. No matter how long or how notably he serves he will never get a commission. He will always be an employee whose job status ends with the last job he holds. There is no status to be obtained by a lifetime of distinguished service that cannot be obtained by five years of routine work. If there is any institutional incentive for the higher civil servant within the civil service system, what is it, and where is it concealed?

It is now coming to be recognized that the federal service is living off of a declining asset, the great infusion of new blood which it received in the 1930's and early 1940's. Two thirds of these men in the higher ranks will have reached retirement age before ten years have passed. The demands upon higher civil servants are increasing; their impact is more critical; yet it seems improbable that they can be replaced with men of equal caliber as they leave the government. In a period of increasing demands for competent administrators at high levels, the prospects are declining, and nothing of significance has been done to meet this need—nothing.

We should face up to an additional fact that capacity and integrity are not enough to make an effective higher civil service. There must be also confidence in the higher civil servant if he is to fulfill his critical mission. His political executive superior must have confidence in him, or he cannot begin to be effective. Congress must have confidence in him if he is not to lack the stability essential to do his job. The public must have confidence in the higher civil service or it will not attract its fair share of the nation's talent—which it very much needs. Most of all, higher civil servants must have confidence in themselves—in their own capacity and integrity. It is obvious that three fourths of the problem of confidence is out of the hands of civil servants themselves. Men can not do their best work if they are mistrusted by their superiors and misunderstood by those whom, ultimately, they serve. The capacity and integrity must be there, to be sure, but also they must be known to be there, not only to the few, but to the many. They must be a matter not only of *expert* knowledge, but of *common* knowledge.

Does such confidence exist today? I do not think so. This is no more than an opinion. You may differ. We lack any recent, valid, and comprehensive measurement. Until one is made we must guess. But from my reading of the signs, the higher civil service falls short in the essential confidence.

Is it possible to raise the civil service as a whole in capacity, in integrity, in dignity, and in status to the place which it deserves, and which the public interest demands, in American life? Yes. But it could take generations for such a glacial change. We need to concentrate our efforts on the critically important *higher* civil service which so largely determines the effectiveness—and the standing—of all the rest.

Is the top management of the government prepared —as a system—to deal with the problems which face it today? I do not think so. We are still unconsciously counting on the time to experiment—which is gone— and on the surplus resources—human as well as material —which have been used up. We cannot afford the mistakes, the delays, and the extravagance which seemed of so little consequence such a short time ago. We are living in what is for us a new and hard world. We must put our adolescence behind us and become as a people political adults. It is time to move vigorously in creating a higher civil service.

5. *How good is*
the best society?

I START WITH THE CONVICTION THAT WE live, here in the United States, not in the ultimate "good society," a Utopia in which all is perfect, but in the best society—the best for man which man yet has been able to devise. The best society is not a perfect society—far from it. It is an imperfect order, but committed to progress, and slowly working toward a condition that will be better than our present best.

I am willing to give reasons for my conviction that we are living in the "best society"; but before doing so it would be desirable to consider some of the criticisms of life in the United States, certain shortcomings of our system, and possible limitations of our political theory.

Criticisms of American Society

It is not hard to draw up an indictment of America today relying exclusively on home-grown critics. One could start with the House Committee on Un-American Activities and its periodic allegations, over the years, that American society is honeycombed with subversion, a serious charge. But of more interest, particularly to men who have received college and university training, are criticisms by intellectuals, men who try to be discerning and critical, but also objective and even scientific, in their approach to American life. Most of these criticisms come not from campus "eggheads" but from men who are working closely (as consultants or through research) with industrial concerns, or who are immersed in business or commercial life. Perhaps we should call these critics the hardboiled eggheads.

The most general criticism is that American life has a damaging effect upon the individual personality, that it is increasingly hostile to individuality. It has been argued for a long time that machine production, for which the assembly line is the symbol, has deprived the American workman of his opportunity for individually creative production. [1] There is doubtless something to this point, although I am not sure that the assembly line is very much different in its demands for conformity than the cotton row or the corn row. I never thought that shocking wheat by hand was so great an expression of my personality that I would not be willing to forego the pleasure. Nature has her own uniformities, and those who work with her must conform. Even so individualistic an activity as milking a cow makes the same demands as does the assembly line

[1] This is perhaps the oldest criticism of the industrial system, and is generally accepted, although it is essentially an inference rather than a conclusion based upon careful and systematic comparisons. It is easy to assume that the "olden days" were better.

T. N. Whitehead's *Leadership in a Free Society* (Cambridge: Harvard University Press, 1936) is an interesting comparison of primitive and industrial economic systems from the point of view of their social satisfactions.

for standardized, repetitive, and, as I recall it, fatigu-ingly monotonous movements. In my experience the only element of variety was introduced by the cow's personality, not mine, and when this became a factor in the situation it never seemed to me to be an improve-ment. I doubt that the laborer has lost much in the way of individual creativity in the factory that he had not already lost in the fields. Planting, cultivating, and reaping are monotonous work, and so is tending live-stock.

If there has been a loss of individual creativity, has it not been in the growth of larger economic units and in the accompanying concentration of planning and directing activities? But here, too, one wonders whether there are proportionately fewer people involved in this than in the good old days. The "overhead" in modern industry is high and the present policy is one of decen-tralizing managing as well as operating functions.

A more recent criticism is that modern life in the United States has deprived man of much of the social satisfaction that he formerly derived from his employ-ment. The social ritual which accompanies productive labor in a primitive society is not present in the austere logic of industrial procedures. It seems to me a little late, however, to cry over this spilt milk. We are a good many generations gone from these rituals. The only recent loss of this sort which we are justified in reckon-ing is that which occurs through reduced group work and through working conditions which do not permit conversation. Whether we are worse off in respect to social satisfactions than our fathers and grandfathers, I do not know (and I doubt that anyone has a very precise or reliable measure of the change).

A variation of this criticism of reduced social satisfaction is that the rapid social change, the fluidity and impermanence of specific industrial procedures, and the mobility of the labor force have destroyed man's sense of security, a security which he derives from a stable or at best slowly changing social context. In other words, he is socially impoverished because of the instability of his specific social context. Elton Mayo, borrowing a concept from Durkheim, feared that many Americans were drifting into a state of *anomie* in which life would be both drab and meaningless. [2]

Thornton Wilder, a sympathetic student of American life, has speculated on what seems to him to be the rootless state of many Americans. [3] They have no geographic "home," no native place which is their subconscious setting, to which they are attached with emotional ties, and from which they presumably draw some sort of spiritual strength. So striking a thought from so sympathetic a critic makes us pause. But we wonder whether Wilder's metaphor may not be misleading. Man is not a vegetable. Not even a tree. And if he be classified with the mammals, he is certainly a very mobile one. I do not know that the plains Indians who

[2] Elton Mayo has argued this point most strongly. See his *Human Problems of an Industrial Civilization*, especially Chap. 6 (New York: Macmillan, 1933). See also Whitehead and F. J. Roethlisberger, *Management and Morale* (Cambridge: Harvard University Press, 1941).

[3] Thornton Wilder, "Toward an American Language," *Atlantic Monthly*, July 1952, pp. 29-37; "The American Loneliness," *Atlantic Monthly*, August 1952, pp. 65-69.

pitched their tepees on a new site every few weeks or
months felt any less at home than the cabin dwellers in
the eastern woodlands who had a fixed abode.

It is generally agreed that social change may be too
slow or too fast, but we have made no effort to find the
optimum (through research) or to determine the range
between too slow and too fast. To take the primitive
society as the benchmark, in my opinion, would be a
serious mistake. There are few modern Americans who
could long endure its confinement, its rigidities, and its
static character.

The latest social critics of the American scene have
felt that the social context is not weak, but too strong.
There are too many "other-directed" persons. They
have lost their capacity to be independent of their
peers. [4] The "organization man" has become the complete captive of the organization, of his own employer,
and of the organized society in which he lives. [5]
Strangely enough this organization man's creator (or
discoverer) is less angry with society than he is with
organization man—for liking it. [6] This in fact is the
burden of Whyte's complaint: the organization man
does *not* feel himself to be a frustrated captive of an

---

[4] See David Riesman's very sympathetic study of modern man's predicament as the subject of a ruthless but unstable peer-group
dictatorship, *The Lonely Crowd* (New Haven: Yale University Press,
1950).

[5] William H. Whyte, Jr., *The Organization Man* (New York: Simon
and Schuster, 1956).

[6] This is my own somewhat subjective reaction to Whyte's most
interesting but also subjective reaction to his cast of characters. See
Whyte's concluding chapter.

overly dominant organization. His most infuriating characteristic is over-adjustment, a feeling that there is no real conflict between himself and the organized society which possesses him. He ought to be unhappy and frustrated; but he isn't. No one could be more relaxed, more at ease with his fellows, and, thinks Whyte, more a lost soul.

Before we grow too much alarmed with the plight of organization man, we should note that this species is concentrated geographically. Its habitat is metropolitan suburbia. This is some assurance; for the species is not yet so dominant in America as it seems to be to men who operate chiefly on the Boston-New York-Washington axis.

A second thought is that it may be as much a mistake to think that there is an inescapable and inherent conflict between man and society, as to think that there is none at all. Author Whyte could be as far away from the truth as his organization man is. The conflict that does exist is a product of the dilemma which is a part of man's nature—the combination of being an individual and of being also a socially molded and socially self-fulfilling individual. The conflict is a product of his desire to be both like his fellows and also different.

At lower levels in the economic order there has been discovered what might be called the "reactive man" or perhaps the "informal-organization man." [7] Industrial psychologists have observed that centralization of direc-

---

[7] The description of the "reactive man" (my term) which follows draws heavily upon Chris Argyris' *Personality and Organization* (New York: Harper, 1958).

tion in industrial organizations and the rigidities of industrial procedures give employees at lower levels little freedom of action.   They are forced into a "dependent, submissive, and passive" role.   It requires of them a response more properly juvenile than adult, leading to frustration and resentment.   The mature worker reacts to this daily attack on his adult personality in a number of ways.   He may try to move up the ladder into a more responsible adult role.   He may move out into another organization in vain hope of escape.   Once thoroughly caught, however, the adult personality reacts with hostility or apathy to compensate for the daily damage to his mature status.   He makes the informal organization a hostile counter force to the formal organization.   He makes demands upon management for compensation or benefits that are essentially a hostile counter blow; for their value and motivation are basically psychological not economic. Such demands are never satisfied, and can't be for they do not fulfill the basic needs which motivated them.

If he does not react hostilely, the frustrated employee may retreat into a shell of apathy.   He does not allow himself to care about his job, his efficiency, or the work situation.   His defense for the hurt to his pride is cynicism, which he also may pass on to his children. He is the future peasant serf of an industrial America.

Efforts of management to overcome hostility or apathy through more directive leadership, paternalism, or propaganda only accentuate the juvenility of the employee's status and increase the intensity of his reactive behavior.   What he would like to forget or change is only made more forceful and obvious to him.

These findings, and they have been too well researched to be ignored, are evidence of a present desire in American society for an adult status of responsible participation. For these frustrated individuals the dignity of man is a personal issue, not an abstract or remote political ideal. The reactive man testifies to the strength and reality of the democratic tradition. These Americans had not expected to grow up to be children. They expected to be men.

The reactive man is no more the typical American than the organization man, but he may be even more numerous, and sufficiently so to be a significant actor on the present scene. It may be hoped that he will continue to make his wants felt, that the signs will be so interpreted that their real meaning is clear, and that remedial measures will go to the heart of the issue, the individual's "adult" status and function in his employment. If the reaction of hostility should become fixed and institutionalized the trend probably would be toward impossibly disruptive labor-management warfare in industry. The trend would be not only regressive economically (in terms of reduced productivity), but the resulting industrial peasantry could not but be costly to social and political democracy as well.

Investigation so far has shown no remedy for the difficulties of the reactive man except his reabsorption into meaningful participation in the decision-making process. Management is now experimenting with much looser supervision, wider delegation of discretion and authority, reduced specialization of labor (which seems to have been carried too far), less "directive" leadership, and employee-oriented supervision rather than production-oriented supervision. [8]   There must be limits as to how far participation can go, but it is significant that such efforts have had some success in meeting the real needs of the reactive man and in increasing productivity.   Is this the beginning of an important management trend?   What are the natural limits of such a movement?   One would like to know, but today it is only possible to guess.

American life in its organizational phases can be criticized on the rather different grounds of "organizational imperialism."   This view is that there is a tendency of economic organizations to push their control over their members farther than is compatible with either individual freedom or with the pluralistic organization which we have thought to characterize American life.   This, it would appear, is what really worries William H. Whyte, Jr.   Eventually when the organization man rises to the executive level, his corporation absorbs him completely. [9]   The fifty to sixty hour week absorbs him physically, and his business problems fill

[8] *Ibid.*, especially Chaps. 7 and 9. See also Rensis Likert, *Developing Patterns of Management,* American Management Association pamphlet, reprinted from General Management Series Nos. 178, 182, 1955, 1956; and *Motivational Dimensions of Administration,* Public Administration Series pamphlet, reprinted from *America's Manpower Crisis;* and "An Emerging Theory of Management Applicable to Public Administration," mimeographed, a paper presented at the Tri-State Management Institute of the American Society For Public Administration, Michigan State University, June 3-7, 1957.

[9] *The Organization Man,* chaps. 11-13.

his thoughts most of his remaining working hours. Wife, children, friends, recreation, religion, and public affairs get little of his attention and none of his real interest. From an organization man he has become "the corporation man" and has given the corporation his all. But if there is compulsion, it is the subtle compulsion of competition. The corporation man likes to work sixty hours a week, he "loves it." If there is a social cost of such a situation it is in the corporate monopolization of a natural leadership group, which is thus lost to public affairs.

Monopolization of its members by the labor union is different; for here the union tries for completeness. The corporation absorbs and can control outside of office hours only "its" men, its top management personnel. The union makes a direct effort to supply the social and political needs of all its members on a broad front. It provides a social life off the job, and it strives for collective bargaining at the polls as well as the conference table. How far these efforts succeed is undetermined. The imperialism appears to be considerably less successful than in the less democratic and more stratified society of England or France. But it is a significant development. Corporations cannot "vote" their employees; this is clear. Such evidence as exists would suggest that there also are limits to labor unions' power to control the votes of their members.

Departing from the strictly economic sphere, a criticism of America is that it does not provide adequate leadership for public affairs. There is no regular source of supply, and no stable group of tested leaders ready to fill even the more important positions which our democratic system, with its so-called checks and balances, requires. Far from having a governing class, men have to be "drafted" for political executive posts in the national government, and since the advent of big government every President has tended to have difficulty in filling important posts with men of the high caliber he desired. The important positions can be filled initially; but it becomes increasingly difficult to keep them filled. There are various explanations: the economic, nonpolitical orientation of the country; 19th century corruption which tarnished "politics" considerably, even in the minds of the corrupters; and the withdrawal of businessmen from politics in the post-Civil War period when the exploitation of resources and rapid industrial expansion in an atmosphere of intense personal competition forced men to choose between business and public affairs. Most businessmen gave up politics, thus depriving an industrial society of its largest natural source of potential leaders.

Whatever the causes, the withdrawal has left a leadership deficit in public affairs for three or four generations. There are signs that the tide may be reversing. Labor's increasing participation in politics since the unions became strong is not improbably a factor. Labor has not supplied many individual leaders for public office, but it has supplied money, organization, and votes (even though the labor vote is not entirely "controlled" by union officials). Business corporations cannot supply votes, and the money which they can supply is not enough. The only thing they have left is leadership skill. The year 1958 may eventually prove to be a landmark—the year when business corporations generally began to reverse their policy of opposing participation in politics by their management personnel, and to encourage it. The Syracuse Chamber of Commerce school for politicians was a new departure, and the experts were guessing that it is symbolic —that there would be a concerted drive to get businessmen into active politics at the grass roots, and that by 1960 the movement would be showing significant results. [10]

There are bound to be mixed feelings about this new effort of business to infiltrate the political parties. But to my way of thinking it will be, in due course, and after some hard lessons, a net public gain. It will be better to have businessmen in politics openly than clandestinely, in responsible official positions than irresponsibly in unofficial positions behind the scenes. The democratic traditions and standards, I believe, are strong enough to condition businessmen no matter how limited or questionable their motives may be for entering politics. To get public support, they will have to make a persuasive case that they are serving the public, not their corporations, and the public will have to be shown.

These home-grown criticisms of American life are in the aggregate a substantial indictment. However one may judge them, it is clear that the best society is not

[10] For a recent report on this trend see the story by Lester Tanzer, "More Companies Edge into Politics . . . ," *Wall Street Journal*, Oct. 14, 1958.

yet as good as it could be. Yet the criticisms also have
their favorable implication; they are evidence of a live
self-critical faculty which is an important characteristic
of American life. [11] The tendency is to take the virtues
of American society for granted, and to worry about its
shortcomings.

Limitations of Political Theory

If the American professional observers and students
of society have discovered some defects in their native
culture, we may be justified in borrowing their critic's
robe long enough to ask whether there may not be some
shortcomings in the critics' theories. Are there limitations in the way the social scientists have approached
the subject? I suggest that possibly some such limitations are observable. Lest you become anxious, I hasten
to add that I shall say nothing about "methodology."
One can only view with enthusiasm the many ingenious
efforts to analyze problems and institutions using new
methods with the hope of getting closer to reality. The
shortcomings to which I refer are to be found not in the
methods but in the assumptions of the social scientists.

1. The first of these is the assumption that man and
society are inherently and inevitably in conflict. Since
I have already argued that American work-a-day doctrines are moving away from this view, my point here is

11 Gunnar Myrdal has commented on the strikingly self critical
qualities which he found to be characteristic of Americans, both social
scientists and laymen. See his *American Dilemma* (New York: Harper,
1944), p. xiii, 22.

that perhaps the theorists have lagged a bit. Some theorists, it seems to me, still tend to assume the existence of an irreducible conflict embedded deep in nature. The existence, in fact, of conflict cannot be denied. But how much of the actual turmoil is unavoidable? How much is a function of nature, and how much is a product of man's haste, ignorance, impatience, and ineptitude? So careful a student of social conflict as Mary Parker Follett argued most persuasively many years ago that the real issues are small in comparison with the turmoil over them. [12] The weight of her argument was that if issues between men and groups are approached early and rationally, goals and policies can be adopted that will meet the real interests of all parties —almost completely. Her experience and her theories of integration, it seems to me, have been passed over too lightly by a subsequent generation of political scientists.

2. A second assumption which seems to me to be open to question is that power (not always defined) is the center and overwhelmingly dominant element of a political system. Isn't political theory too much obsessed with power as a phenomenon? This despite the fact that in Western Christendom, physical force and even economic compulsion seem to be receding as observable forces in day-to-day living.

Power is certainly important, no one can deny it; but is it any more central to the existence of society than mutual benefit, associational satisfactions, or good will?

[12] This theme comes out in many of her essays. See Henry C. Metcalf and L. Urwick, *Dynamic Administration, The Collected Papers of Mary Parker Follett* (New York: Harper, 1942).

It may be argued, I think, that the only social function of force is to control force. That is, the function of authority (with its ultimate sanctions of force) is to prevent the arbitrary resolution of social as well as individual problems by violence. Force is not even able to hold the police state together despite its very extensive use. An invading conqueror of old could rule a conquered land for a time; but what held his conquering bands together? It was something more than raw force. In modern dictatorships of the Soviet or Fascist type, where a few have conquered the many from the inside, the army and the police are forceful agents in governing; and the secret police keep the army and the ordinary police in line. Above the secret police may be a higher and more secret police, but somewhere unity must be achieved by other means than force. Political science is more than the study of power.

3. A third fault of political theory, I suggest, is its neglect of the element of sacrifice. If there is any validity to the point which I have tried to make (in Chapter 2, on Society) that no society has ever been operated without sacrifice, that one aspect of progress is to reduce the amount of sacrifice, and that an important aspect of democracy is to make increasing reliance upon voluntary sacrifice, then sacrifice as an element in the fabric of society deserves more attention than the political theorists have given it.

4. A fourth possible defect of political science is its failure to appreciate the force of democratic momentum. We are aware of dual streams of ideas and ideals in Western culture. For every democratic ideal there is a

more or less submerged counterpart that challenges it squarely. The dominance of the "higher" ideal over the "lower" has not been achieved easily or quickly. It has been achieved inch by inch in an unending struggle to mold men and institutions. At times progress has been slow and the battle desperate. There also have been disastrous times when an ingenious demagogue exploiting the distress of a people has been able to make the subversive anti-democratic ideology dominant, and to submerge democratic theory, driving it underground. The demise of Hitler and Mussolini is too recent for us to have forgotten their monstrous successes and the monumental disasters which they have bequeathed to civilization as a lasting moral burden. We even have humbler examples nearer at hand of the demagogue's ability to appeal to the subversive ideology which challenges the basic principles of American democracy, and to get away with it. We have in our discussions (Chapter 1) pondered those aspects of man's being which make him susceptible to such disastrous enchantment. More important than any of these ominous facts, however, is the momentum which democracy generates. As it succeeds, its ideals become more compelling. The more democratic a society becomes, the more it is compelled to go ahead toward its democratic goals. There is a spiral force here that works upward with cumulative effect. A people which has not experienced democracy does not have a very great desire for it. A taste of democracy, when there has been genuine experience with it, whets the appetite for more, and so the democratic drive develops. Probably after it has gained real momentum the democratic drive can be stopped only by some form of revolutionary violence from a dissident faction; for once the premises of democracy are accepted, its logic is irrefutable.

We should have understood this phenomenon from our own experience, even without the 1956 demonstrations of Russia's satellite states. This is perhaps the great dilemma of Russian politics. How much freedom, how much deference to the individual, how much fair and honest debate, and how much participation in government can the powers-that-be permit without letting democratic forces get out of hand? Apparently, not much! If these forces were allowed to spiral upward a bit they would break the bonds of the authoritarian system.

Should we not face the probability, also, that if the democratic momentum is stopped by a sufficiently forceful act, it will reverse? The benefits and values of a democratic society will be undermined one by one; and the powers-that-be will move regressively toward more irrational and more authoritarian methods. It would appear that a civilized people must move in one direction or the other. It cannot stand still. Short of revolution, a people committed to democracy have no choice except as to pace and method. I wish that the political scientists had helped us to understand this democratic momentum and had prepared us for its implications.

5. A fifth limitation of political science is its tendency to work with too small an area of political life on the apparent assumption that it is a whole unit. Frag-

ments and parts have thus been treated as wholes. As no individual can long exist or be understood apart from his family, his friends, and the circles in which he moves, so also no city, no state or province, and no nation can be understood apart from the broader society of which it is a part. A political theory based upon the traditional concept of national sovereignty is not very realistic as an analytical device, and it has become impossibly dangerous as a basis for operating policy. Perhaps the smallest whole society is a civilization, or it may be that nothing short of the wide world will do. [13] One could argue the matter. But from all the signs of both past and present, it would appear to be wise to construe the bounds of Western Civilization very liberally, and to be prepared to assume at some not too distant time that there is only one whole society on Earth. If we can make this adjustment in our thinking, we may get a little closer to reality and may avoid some egregious errors in public policy.

6. Finally I question the tacit assumption of political science that a political system in an advanced society is or can be self-contained. We have accepted as a practical matter the interpenetration of economic and political activity; we are aware of the associational satisfactions which men seek in all activity; and we note large areas of conventional or non-rational behavior; but it does not seem to me that we have yet absorbed these data into our thinking about government. There is still an assumption that a system can be devised that

[13] See Toynbee, *A Study of History.*

will be at least semi-automatic, living on its own momentum, a kind of Atmos clock that absorbs enough energy from the changing temperature to turn its wheels indefinitely.   Is not this assumption most unreal?

All of the systems of behavior in a society are inter-related.   Each draws something from the other and gives something to the other.   But there is friction in all, and there is constant obsolescence in all.   Whence comes the power to compensate for the friction, and the creativity to overcome obsolescence?

We have noted the phenomena of sacrifice, especially voluntary sacrifice, and creative leadership.   But what produces the willingness to sacrifice, and what generates the compulsion to create.   I know of no constitution which provides for these elements, nor are they products of any political institution with which I am familiar. They come from the minds and hearts of men.   But what puts them there?   Do you know?   I don't.   Does anyone know?   I don't think so.

These elements of sacrifice and creativity, essential to the progress of an advanced democratic society, come from within man.   Perhaps we should simply accept the psychoanalytic view of man's basic bipolarity, his "death wish" and his "creative drives," and say that the capacity for sacrifice and the capacity for creativity are the very essence of man's nature, and that the creative sacrifice is the highest of all human fulfillments.   This may be of some help intellectually; it may give us some assurance; but as political scientists desiring to assist in evolving institutions which will increase the probability of survival and progress, we get little guidance from these concepts. What can be done to make sure that the latent capacity in man's nature will lead to socially adequate performance by flesh-and-blood men and women in specific situations? That is the question.

Society can recognize, honor, and reward constructive sacrifice and creative leadership, and this is a matter to which Americans may now need to give thought. But political action can neither create nor develop these qualities in man. The most that can be done governmentally is to protect and support the institutions which do tend to develop these qualities: the family, the church, and the democratic public school system. These activities are already established in public policy. The most important effect of many activities in the field of municipal functions—law-and-order activities, public utility services, and social security services—is to safeguard healthy family life. But the state cannot even support the church in providing religious instruction without weakening it; it can only guarantee religious freedom. Its major direct contribution has been the democratic system of free public schools. But even here, government can only provide the framework. It can build school houses, and it can provide teacher's colleges and universities where prospective teachers acquire knowledge of subjects and useful educational procedures. But from what source comes the interest in other human beings, the warmth, and the joy in learning which binds teachers and students together in an active process of growth? Without these qualities in the teachers, particularly in the student's early years, not much happens educationally; and it is beyond the power of either the teacher's college or the university to put these qualities into teachers. They have already been developed by prior teachers, religious and secular, and by parents. And have not these parents and early teachers worked with qualities which were already there, ready to be cultivated, when they first met the child?

The point is that although it is essential that society do everything possible to bring out in its members capacity for creative leadership and constructive sacrifice, the development of these essentials is largely beyond the reach of political action, and their implantation is presently beyond all human action. Will the right men come forward at the right time to overcome the frictions of minor mistakes, to absorb the shock of egregious error, and to prune and graft the living social structure so that it can grow and flourish? We political scientists do not know. All we can say is that this important question is beyond the reach of political theory. The progress of an advancing society requires an "input" that is beyond the power of political scientists to predict and perhaps beyond the power of the social *system* to assure.

Why the Best Society?

After reviewing the criticisms of American society and the limitations of political theory, we should now consider the proposition that American society is the best for man so far devised.

It is best, first of all because of its democratic qualities (discussed more fully in Chapter 2, "Is Democracy Viable?"): (a) That is, no other system so well accommodates both the affiliative and the individualistic tendencies of man. (b) No other system provides such great opportunities for individual growth. Not only are there widespread opportunities for growth, but no other society stimulates great growth by expecting so much of man as does democracy. (c) The growth so stimulated, moreover, is more likely to include abundant and mature leadership than in a nondemocratic society.

Although the United States of America is not a complete society, but is a portion of a wider society, it is a significant portion with some peculiar virtues of its own, which, I think, enhance its attributes as the best society.

1. In America people do have a serious and continuing concern with the relations of individuals and society. This is an important part of our constitutional law. It has also an important place in American literature and American social studies. Moral ideals also play an important place in American thinking about individual adjustments, which is some assurance that the hard lessons of long experience will not be lost. Without these moral standards would there be the concern with preserving the individual's integrity that both humanists and social scientists exhibit in America? These convictions are so deep that they are perhaps taken for granted and overlooked by Americans.

One of the most thorough and best informed European students of the United States has said that

"Americans of all national origins, classes, creeds, and colors have something in common; a social ethos, a political creed. It is difficult to avoid the judgment that this American creed is the cement in the structure of this great and disparate nation. . . . America compared to every other country in Western civilization . . . has the most explicitly expressed system of general ideals in reference to human relations. This body of ideals is more widely understood and appreciated than similar ideals are elsewhere. . . . The creed has been made conscious to everyone in American society. . . . The ideals of the essential dignity of the individual human being, of the fundamental equality of all men, and of certain inalienable rights to freedom, justice, and a fair opportunity represent to the American people the essential meaning of the nation's struggle for independence." [14] If this view is correct, and I think it is, it is not surprising that America has made and is making substantial progress toward full realization of these ideals.

2. American society does give great weight to reason. We are a self critical people, and we are given to open criticism. [15] We also believe in education, universal education, and have carried our system of free public schools farther than any other people. The Soviet Union may be challenging our educational pre-eminence; but there is no doubt that we have been the leader among Western nations. Our commitment to reasonable methods and a reasonable approach is strong.

[14] Myrdal, p. 3.
[15] *Ibid.*, p. xiii.

3. There is good will in American society. This is its characteristic mood, not hatred. Overt evidence of this good will is worth noting—for example, American philanthropy. There is nothing like it anywhere else. In no other land are there professional bureaucracies created to give away hundreds of millions of dollars every year; and these investments in good works are dwarfed by the unorganized charitable contributions of millions of ordinary men and women. The system of privately supported colleges, a peculiar American institution, is also a monument to good will. (But one must note that the largest contributors to their support are their faculties who have sacrificed what they might have earned in other professions in order to continue teaching.) The generous response of Americans to human want at home or abroad is well known. Still more fundamental is the friendliness and "Christian neighborliness" of Americans. [16] I think it is more in evidence in the smaller cities and villages than in the great urban centers where good manners are not the standard behavior of man in the mass; but the neighborliness is there, and emerges once the anonymity of the mass is broken.

4. There is leadership in American life in rather large supply, although it is not presently channeled into government. Reluctant but responsible men do come forward to organize and lead group efforts in behalf of public causes, ranging from the trivial to the noblest conceivable. Voluntary associations seem to spring to

16 *Ibid.*, p. 11.

life equipped with officers, committees, secretaries, volunteer workers, and a will to do battle for right, justice, the underdog, and "our side." There is probably enough organizing talent devoted to health enterprises alone in the United States to settle many of the World's problems if it could only be focused upon them. Consider the national organizations which divide the human body among them in their efforts to cope with tuberculosis, cancer, heart disease, infantile paralysis, multiple sclerosis, muscular dystrophy, and mental disorders. Health is by no means unique. Other areas have their array of voluntary organizations: social work, recreation, "conservation," and foreign policy. The array is formidable even without getting into the multitude of groups which have a particular economic interest to promote or defend.

Recapitulating, the society in which we live is best for man because it is democratic, and so offers man maximum opportunity to reach his fullest development. Beyond this, America's especial concern for the individual in his relation to society, its commitment to reason, its basic good will, and the abundance of leadership talent and opportunities enrich America's democratic character and strengthen the probability that it will survive and continue to be progressively democratic.

Limitations of the Best Society

Even the best society so far devised falls short of man's hopes and present-day Americans are well aware of limitations in their own world. If we were to attempt to apply our two standards (pragmatic and predictive) to American life, what would we find?

Applying the pragmatic standard first, considering past and present performance, what does it show? In municipal functions, the national imperative, the personal imperative, and the international imperative, what is the situation? Let me suggest some very general and tentative propositions for your consideration.

In the matter of municipal functions, it seems to me, we would find neither great strength nor great weakness. In the past we have done an adequate, but not a distinguished job. The real test is coming up. How will we deal with the accelerating urban growth? Will we be able to meet the needs of people in metropolitan areas by rational measures so that conditions of life will improve, or will the costs, individual and public, of urban living mount while the amenities decline? Before we leap to an optimistic conclusion, let us remember that when portal-to-portal time is included, many commuters are working a twelve-hour day; and possibly most of them are more hours away from home than were their fathers and grandfathers. As yet there has been no real "break-through" in the solution of metropolitan problems.

In the public utility functions our record is on the whole respectable, and it is outstanding in the field of public education, where we have some problems on our hands at the moment. The most difficult of these, it seems to me is not the matter of desegregation which is getting the most publicity (I am sure it will be solved) but the one which is getting no attention at all. This is the predicament of the children with superior intellectual ability who have to spend twelve years in the public schools, four years in college, two to four years as officers in the armed forces, and from two to six years longer to complete their professional training. In all, these men spend from twenty to twenty-six years in formal education (including military service). Many of them are our ablest men intellectually. This is too long a period for them to be in school, too long for their own best development, and too long for the country's good. We have improved our system of education by extending it. The educational tree has been fertilized, and it has flourished, but it has not been pruned. It is possible that if the means of avoiding this wastage, which already have been tested, were put into general use they could cut three or four years out of the twenty to twenty-six years of formal schooling; and I think that the quality of education would actually be improved in the process. On this problem I am pessimistic; I fear that reform will be slow.

In handling "welfare state" activities our record seems to me to be average, nothing to be alarmed about and nothing to brag about. I don't see difficulties coming up that cannot be handled.

Taking the municipal functions as a whole, we show normal capacity for an advanced nation. The volume operations and the technical problems are not particularly difficult, but neither have we given any of these functions major attention. We have difficulties facing us in making progressive adjustments in metropolitan government and in education, which will require imagination and creative leadership for their solution. Do we have it?

Despite their importance, we need not dwell long on the "national imperatives" of defense and "full employment." In the defense area we are encountering, for the first time in our national history, professional bureaucracies which are both great and powerful, with potent allies in the committees of Congress, and in the industrial world. In this interplay of forces where there are desperate institutional rivalries, can facts be faced honestly, can issues be settled on their merits? Or, will rational thinking be twisted into unrealistic and extravagant decisions? This is a new test for the rational capacities of American government. It is by no means clear that we will be able to meet it. There is also great danger that in the heat of controversy and as a result of bureaucratically stimulated anxiety, "defense" will be conceived too narrowly as a military matter. This could be fatal.

In meeting the "full employment" imperative we note encouraging progress, but limited perhaps more by the inadequacy of doctrines than by the machinery of government. We note also much more public concern with the consequences of deflation than of inflation. Is this a reasonable approach? Or are we headed for the same sort of painful lesson on the subject of inflation that we suffered on the topic of unemployment in the Great Depression? One could guess that with reference to the economic imperative we have enough competence or will learn fast enough to escape disaster, but that we shall lose some skin and get some severe bruises in the process. Or is this too optimistic a view?

In the personal imperative we score best on the pragmatic test I think—very well in fact. Our one weak spot is a lack of perception in dealing with the subtle problems of minorities. Has this not been a factor in absorbing every immigrant group that has come to our shores? Have we ever really understood the minority's feelings, its values, its difficult position? Has there not been undue and unnecessary hardship? The most striking example of failure is not the Negro, but the American Indian. There has not been satisfactory progress from any point of view—Indian or non-Indian. The largest single cause of failure, I believe, is the unwillingness or inability to understand and accept as realities the Indian's values, standards, goals and philosophy. We dealt with an assumed Indian, not the real Indian, and we got nowhere. This failure in dealing with domestic minorities which are culturally different, suggests possibly ominous weakness in meeting the international imperative. The cultures of the Asians and Africans are quite different from ours, and in the world's population we are the minority, not they. There are also important, although not such extreme differences, in the cultures of North and South America. If we fail to understand the psychology and the sociology of these people on other continents, we are almost certain to come to grief in trying to help them make economic and political progress. *Their* philosophy will govern their reactions to us and to world situations, not *our* philosophy. Yet we seem not very well prepared for, or accustomed to, dealing with this kind of reality, or even conscious of its importance. In this area I am inclined to be pessimistic for the immediate future. Although we may learn fast, the lessons are bound to be painful.

If we turn now to the predictive index and try to use it to throw light on the causes of the "best society's" limitations, what clues do we get? I should like to add only two points to those made earlier (in discussion of goals, doctrines, rationality of political structures, leadership and authority). The first is that the weaknesses on these points although they are not numerous, are serious in that each one accentuates others, compounding the total effect.

The unrealistic doctrines about the nature and role of government, the rational defects in legislative institutions (aspects of legislative composition, organization, and procedure which do not maximize rational decisions in the public interest), and the failure of government to get its due share of the reasonably abundant leadership talent which is developed in America are not unrelated to each other. They also are related to the weaknesses in setting public goals, and to the vital authority of American society. If the doctrines regarding government were realistic, would not government get more of the best talent which society produces? Would not it be more likely that the irrationalities of the legislative process would be corrected? Would not we have more challenging and realistic public goals? And would not government act with greater moral force and vigor at home and also abroad? As Barnard has noted, a great danger which democracy faces is a "tyranny of indecision." [17] Better compelling moral force any day, than this awful taskmaster.

Although goals for the individual seem adequate, except that they may be too limited to economic and political affairs, public goals and goal fixing leave something to be desired. Increasingly, individual needs can be satisfied only through joint action. The public goals to guide joint action, however, too often are at best vague or casual. For example, millions of men, women, and children enjoy and benefit from outdoor life in forested and wilderness areas. But only a few score individuals can have forested estates. The many millions must depend upon public parks, public forests, and public recreation areas. Have adequate public goals been established? I am not aware of them. In urban America, what are our public goals for the metropolis a decade hence? Can anyone tell us what they are? And without goals what kind of a metropolis will we have?

As to the international imperative, what are American goals? Is our objective merely to meet one crisis after another with counter measures, letting the initiative rest with others? Do we have a more positive goal of anticipating and minimizing specific problems that otherwise are likely to arise? Or is it our goal to get beyond the problem approach and to promote such generally healthful world conditions that serious inter-

[17] Chester Barnard, *Organization and Management* (Cambridge: Harvard University Press, 1948), p. 47.

national maladies do not occur? In the public health field, public policy moved from quarantine of epidemic disease, to preventive immunization, and finally to positive health building programs. Where are we in dealing with the health of the world order?

The second point concerning the predictive or analytical index is that somewhere, somehow, in our doctrines, in our political theory, in our efforts to face the political realities of the world, we have overlooked good will as an element in American life and as a political force in society. Is it not one of the most, if not *the* most, important unifying forces in all groups—the family, the community, the nation, and civilization? There are other factors to be sure, some of which have been at times considered to be the decisive element: force, reason, and mutual benefit. But is there ever real unity, real solidarity, without good will?

This may well be America's greatest strength and its most valuable asset in coping with the problems of progress and survival. Why be ashamed of this attribute of the American culture? Why is it necessary to justify every appropriation for what we are afraid to call "foreign aid" on grounds of immediate military or economic return? If as we now well know, people inevitably create an informal organization as a counterpart to every formal organization, if the grievances which are at the seat of most economic disputes between labor and management are psychological and social, not economic (and this has been documented many times over), if political bosses have based "corrupt" political machines on the bedrock of friendship and personal favors, and if the vital principal of American politics is personal confidence, surely it is reasonable to give official recognition to the factor of good will as a unifying and constructive force in a democratic society. The greatest need and the greatest opportunity before America today may well be to find ways and means of infusing the acts and the processes of government with the good will which permeates a democratic culture at least in latent form, and which in large part motivates much that a democratic people try to accomplish through government.

It is important in domestic affairs. No family can flourish or long survive without releasing the affections of its members. How can the state afford to ignore this principle? Why cannot all of the municipal functions be permeated with good will?

In any walk of life, private or public, at home or abroad, whoever won friends by making men afraid of him? (Hostility begets hostility.) . . . By handing out gratuities? (No one likes to receive alms of a stranger.) . . . By displaying his wealth, his strength, his engineering skill, or his knowledge of nuclear physics? (No one loves an exhibitionist but his mother!) . . . There is a place for all of these activities but they do not bring people together in a united community.

I suggest that we re-evaluate the forgotten asset of good will and put it to work more actively in America and for America—and for the world.

Index